The Private life, T[he] time, Lord Beaupré, [...] Collaboration, Owen Wingrave

Henry James

Alpha Editions

This edition published in 2024

ISBN 9789362510600

Design and Setting By
Alpha Editions
www.alphaedis.com
Email - info@alphaedis.com

As per information held with us this book is in Public Domain.
This book is a reproduction of an important historical work.
Alpha Editions uses the best technology to reproduce historical work
in the same manner it was first published to preserve its original nature.
Any marks or number seen are left intentionally to preserve.

Contents

THE PRIVATE LIFE	- 1 -
THE WHEEL OF TIME	- 31 -
I	- 32 -
II	- 39 -
III	- 48 -
IV	- 53 -
V	- 58 -
VI	- 65 -
LORD BEAUPRÉ	- 72 -
I	- 73 -
II	- 81 -
III	- 89 -
IV	- 100 -
V	- 106 -
VI	- 115 -
THE VISITS	- 124 -
COLLABORATION	- 138 -
OWEN WINGRAVE	- 156 -
I	- 157 -
II	- 162 -
III	- 170 -
IV	- 180 -

THE PRIVATE LIFE

We talked of London, face to face with a great bristling, primeval glacier. The hour and the scene were one of those impressions which make up a little, in Switzerland, for the modern indignity of travel—the promiscuities and vulgarities, the station and the hotel, the gregarious patience, the struggle for a scrappy attention, the reduction to a numbered state. The high valley was pink with the mountain rose, the cool air as fresh as if the world were young. There was a faint flush of afternoon on undiminished snows, and the fraternizing tinkle of the unseen cattle came to us with a cropped and sun-warmed odour. The balconied inn stood on the very neck of the sweetest pass in the Oberland, and for a week we had had company and weather. This was felt to be great luck, for one would have made up for the other had either been bad.

The weather certainly would have made up for the company; but it was not subjected to this tax, for we had by a happy chance the *fleur des pois*. Lord and Lady Mellifont, Clare Vawdrey, the greatest (in the opinion of many) of our literary glories, and Blanche Adney, the greatest (in the opinion of all) of our theatrical. I mention these first, because they were just the people whom in London, at that time, people tried to "get." People endeavoured to "book" them six weeks ahead, yet on this occasion we had come in for them, we had all come in for each other, without the least wire-pulling. A turn of the game had pitched us together, the last of August, and we recognized our luck by remaining so, under protection of the barometer. When the golden days were over—that would come soon enough—we should wind down opposite sides of the pass and disappear over the crest of surrounding heights. We were of the same general communion, we participated in the same miscellaneous publicity. We met, in London, with irregular frequency; we were more or less governed by the laws and the language, the traditions and the shibboleths of the same dense social state. I think all of us, even the ladies, "did" something, though we pretended we didn't when it was mentioned. Such things are not mentioned indeed in London, but it was our innocent pleasure to be different here. There had to be some way to show the difference, inasmuch as we were under the impression that this was our annual holiday. We felt at any rate that the conditions were more human than in London, or that at least we ourselves were. We were frank about this, we talked about it: it was what we were talking about as we looked at the flushing glacier, just as some one called attention to the prolonged absence of Lord Mellifont and Mrs. Adney. We were seated on the terrace of the inn, where there were benches and little tables, and those of us who were most bent on proving that we had returned to nature were, in the queer Germanic fashion, having coffee before meat.

The remark about the absence of our two companions was not taken up, not even by Lady Mellifont, not even by little Adney, the fond composer; for it had been dropped only in the briefest intermission of Clare Vawdrey's talk. (This celebrity was "Clarence" only on the title-page.) It was just that revelation of our being after all human that was his theme. He asked the company whether, candidly, every one hadn't been tempted to say to every one else: "I had no idea you were really so nice." I had had, for my part, an idea that he was, and even a good deal nicer, but that was too complicated to go into then; besides it is exactly my story. There was a general understanding among us that when Vawdrey talked we should be silent, and not, oddly enough, because he at all expected it. He didn't, for of all abundant talkers he was the most unconscious, the least greedy and professional. It was rather the religion of the host, of the hostess, that prevailed among us: it was their own idea, but they always looked for a listening circle when the great novelist dined with them. On the occasion I allude to there was probably no one present with whom, in London, he had not dined, and we felt the force of this habit. He had dined even with me; and on the evening of that dinner, as on this Alpine afternoon, I had been at no pains to hold my tongue, absorbed as I inveterately was in a study of the question which always rose before me, to such a height, in his fair, square, strong stature.

This question was all the more tormenting that he never suspected himself (I am sure) of imposing it, any more than he had ever observed that every day of his life every one listened to him at dinner. He used to be called "subjective" in the weekly papers, but in society no distinguished man could have been less so. He never talked about himself; and this was a topic on which, though it would have been tremendously worthy of him, he apparently never even reflected. He had his hours and his habits, his tailor and his hatter, his hygiene and his particular wine, but all these things together never made up an attitude. Yet they constituted the only attitude he ever adopted, and it was easy for him to refer to our being "nicer" abroad than at home. *He* was exempt from variations, and not a shade either less or more nice in one place than in another. He differed from other people, but never from himself (save in the extraordinary sense which I will presently explain), and struck me as having neither moods nor sensibilities nor preferences. He might have been always in the same company, so far as he recognized any influence from age or condition or sex: he addressed himself to women exactly as he addressed himself to men, and gossiped with all men alike, talking no better to clever folk than to dull. I used to feel a despair at his way of liking one subject—so far as I could tell—precisely as much as another: there were some I hated so myself. I never found him anything but loud and cheerful and copious, and I never heard him utter a paradox or express a shade or play with an idea. That fancy about our being "human" was, in his conversation, quite an exceptional flight. His opinions were sound and second-rate, and of his perceptions it was too mystifying to think. I envied him his magnificent health.

Vawdrey had marched, with his even pace and his perfectly good conscience, into the flat country of anecdote, where stories are visible from afar like windmills and signposts; but I observed after a little that Lady Mellifont's attention wandered. I happened to be sitting next her. I noticed that her eyes rambled a little anxiously over the lower slopes of the mountains. At last, after looking at her watch, she said to me: "Do you know where they went?"

"Do you mean Mrs. Adney and Lord Mellifont?"

"Lord Mellifont and Mrs. Adney." Her ladyship's speech seemed—unconsciously indeed—to correct me, but it didn't occur to me that this was because she was jealous. I imputed to her no such vulgar sentiment: in the first place, because I liked her, and in the second because it would always occur to one quickly that it was right, in any connection, to put Lord Mellifont first. He *was* first—extraordinarily first. I don't say greatest or wisest or most renowned, but essentially at the top of the list and the head of the table. That is a position by itself, and his wife was naturally accustomed to see him in it. My phrase had sounded as if Mrs. Adney had taken him; but it was not possible for him to be taken—he only took. No one, in the nature of things, could know this better than Lady Mellifont. I had originally been rather afraid of her, thinking her, with her stiff silences and the extreme blackness of almost everything that made up her person, somewhat hard, even a little saturnine. Her paleness seemed slightly grey, and her glossy black hair metallic, like the brooches and bands and combs with which it was inveterately adorned. She was in perpetual mourning, and wore numberless ornaments of jet and onyx, a thousand clicking chains and bugles and beads. I had heard Mrs. Adney call her the queen of night, and the term was descriptive if you understood that the night was cloudy. She had a secret, and if you didn't find it out as you knew her better you at least perceived that she was gentle and unaffected and limited, and also rather submissively sad. She was like a woman with a painless malady. I told her that I had merely seen her husband and his companion stroll down the glen together about an hour before, and suggested that Mr. Adney would perhaps know something of their intentions.

Vincent Adney, who, though he was fifty years old, looked like a good little boy on whom it had been impressed that children should not talk before company, acquitted himself with remarkable simplicity and taste of the position of husband of a great exponent of comedy. When all was said about her making it easy for him, one couldn't help admiring the charmed affection with which he took everything for granted. It is difficult for a husband who is not on the stage, or at least in the theatre, to be graceful about a wife who is; but Adney was more than graceful—he was exquisite, he was inspired. He set his beloved to music; and you remember how genuine his music could be—the only English compositions I ever saw a foreigner take an interest in. His wife was in them, somewhere, always; they were like a free, rich translation of the impression she produced. She seemed, as one listened, to pass laughing, with loosened hair, across the scene. He had been only a little fiddler at her theatre, always in his place during the acts; but she had made him something rare and misunderstood. Their superiority had become a kind of partnership, and their happiness was a part of the happiness of their friends. Adney's one discomfort was that he couldn't write a play for his wife, and the only way he meddled with her affairs was by asking impossible people if *they* couldn't.

Lady Mellifont, after looking across at him a moment, remarked to me that she would rather not put any question to him. She added the next minute: "I had rather people shouldn't see I'm nervous."

"*Are* you nervous?"

"I always become so if my husband is away from me for any time."

"Do you imagine something has happened to him?"

"Yes, always. Of course I'm used to it."

"Do you mean his tumbling over precipices—that sort of thing?"

"I don't know exactly what it is: it's the general sense that he'll never come back."

She said so much and kept back so much that the only way to treat the condition she referred to seemed the jocular. "Surely he'll never forsake you!" I laughed.

She looked at the ground a moment. "Oh, at bottom I'm easy."

"Nothing can ever happen to a man so accomplished, so infallible, so armed at all points," I went on, encouragingly.

"Oh, you don't know how he's armed!" she exclaimed, with such an odd quaver that I could account for it only by her being nervous. This idea was confirmed by her moving just afterwards, changing her seat rather pointlessly, not as if to cut our conversation short, but because she was in a fidget. I couldn't know what was the matter with her, but I was presently relieved to see Mrs. Adney come toward us. She had in her hand a big bunch of wild flowers, but she was not closely attended by Lord Mellifont. I quickly saw, however, that she had no disaster to announce; yet as I knew there was a question Lady Mellifont would like to hear answered, but did not wish to ask, I expressed to her immediately the hope that his lordship had not remained in a crevasse.

"Oh, no; he left me but three minutes ago. He has gone into the house." Blanche Adney rested her eyes on mine an instant—a mode of intercourse to which no man, for himself, could ever object. The interest, on this occasion, was quickened by the particular thing the eyes happened to say. What they usually said was only: "Oh, yes, I'm charming, I know, but don't make a fuss about it. I only want a new part—I do, I do!" At present they added, dimly, surreptitiously, and of course sweetly—for that was the way they did everything: "It's all right, but something did happen. Perhaps I'll tell you later." She turned to Lady Mellifont, and the transition to simple gaiety suggested her mastery of her profession. "I've brought him safe. We had a charming walk."

"I'm so very glad," returned Lady Mellifont, with her faint smile; continuing vaguely, as she got up: "He must have gone to dress for dinner. Isn't it rather near?" She moved away, to the hotel, in her leave-taking, simplifying fashion, and the rest of us, at the mention of dinner, looked at each other's watches, as if to shift the responsibility of such grossness. The head-waiter, essentially, like all head-waiters, a man of the world, allowed us hours and places of our own, so that in the evening, apart under the lamp, we formed a compact, an indulged little circle. But it was only the Mellifonts who "dressed" and as to whom it was recognized that they naturally *would* dress: she in exactly the same manner as on any other evening of her ceremonious existence (she was not a woman whose habits could take account of anything so mutable as fitness); and he, on the other hand, with remarkable adjustment and suitability. He was almost as much a man of the world as the head-waiter, and spoke almost as many languages; but he abstained from courting a comparison of dress-coats and white waistcoats, analyzing the occasion in a much finer way—into black velvet and blue velvet and brown velvet, for instance, into delicate harmonies of necktie and subtle informalities of shirt. He had a costume for every function and a moral for every costume; and his functions and costumes and morals were ever a part of the amusement of life—a part at any rate of its beauty and romance— for an immense circle of spectators. For his particular friends indeed these things were more than an amusement; they were a topic, a social support and of course, in addition, a subject of perpetual suspense. If his wife had not been present before dinner they were what the rest of us probably would have been putting our heads together about.

Clare Vawdrey had a fund of anecdote on the whole question: he had known Lord Mellifont almost from the beginning. It was a peculiarity of this nobleman that there could be no conversation about him that didn't instantly take the form of anecdote, and a still further distinction that there could apparently be no anecdote that was not on the whole to his honour. If he had come into a room at any moment, people might have said frankly: "Of course we were telling stories about you!" As consciences go, in London, the general conscience would have been good. Moreover it would have been impossible to imagine his taking such a tribute otherwise than amiably, for he was always as unperturbed as an actor with the right cue. He had never in his life needed the prompter—his very embarrassments had been rehearsed. For myself, when he was talked about I always had an odd impression that we were speaking of the dead—it was with that peculiar accumulation of relish. His reputation was a kind of gilded obelisk, as if he had been buried beneath it; the body of legend and reminiscence of which he was to be the subject had crystallized in advance.

This ambiguity sprang, I suppose, from the fact that the mere sound of his name and air of his person, the general expectation he created, were, somehow, too exalted to be verified. The experience of his urbanity always came later; the prefigurement, the legend paled before the reality. I remember that on the evening I refer to the reality was particularly operative. The handsomest man of his period could never have looked better, and he sat among us like a bland conductor controlling by an harmonious play of arm an orchestra still a little rough. He directed the conversation by gestures as irresistible as they were vague; one felt as if without him it wouldn't have had anything to call a tone. This was essentially what he contributed to any occasion—what he contributed above all to English public life. He pervaded it, he coloured it, he embellished it, and without him it would scarcely have had a vocabulary. Certainly it would not have had a style; for a style was what it had in having Lord Mellifont. He *was* a style. I was freshly struck with it as, in the *salle à manger* of the little Swiss inn, we resigned ourselves to inevitable veal. Confronted with his form (I must parenthesize that it was not confronted much), Clare Vawdrey's talk suggested the reporter contrasted with the bard. It was interesting to watch the shock of characters from which, of an evening, so much would be expected. There was however no concussion— it was all muffled and minimized in Lord Mellifont's tact. It was rudimentary with him to find the solution of such a problem in playing the host, assuming responsibilities which carried with them their sacrifice. He had indeed never been a guest in his life; he was the host, the patron, the moderator at every board. If there was a defect in his manner (and I suggest it under my breath), it was that he had a little more art than any conjunction—even the most complicated—could possibly require. At any rate one made one's reflections in noticing how the accomplished peer handled the situation and how the sturdy man of letters was unconscious that the situation (and least of all he himself as part of it), was handled. Lord Mellifont poured forth treasures of tact, and Clare Vawdrey never dreamed he was doing it.

Vawdrey had no suspicion of any such precaution even when Blanche Adney asked him if he saw yet their third act—an inquiry into which she introduced a subtlety of her own. She had a theory that he was to write her a play and that the heroine, if he would only do his duty, would be the part for which she had immemorially longed. She was forty years old (this could be no secret to those who had admired her from the first), and she could now reach out her hand and touch her uttermost goal. This gave a kind of tragic passion—perfect actress of comedy as she was—to her desire not to miss the great thing. The years had passed, and still she had missed it; none of the things she had done was the thing she had dreamed of, so that at present there was no more time to lose. This was the canker in the rose, the ache beneath the smile. It made her touching—made her sadness even sweeter than her laughter. She had done the old English and the new French, and had charmed her generation; but she was haunted by the vision of a bigger chance, of something truer to the conditions that lay near her. She was tired of Sheridan and she hated Bowdler; she called for a canvas of a finer grain. The worst of it, to my sense, was that she would never extract her modern comedy from the great mature novelist, who was as incapable of producing it as he was of threading a needle. She coddled him, she talked to him, she made love to him, as she frankly proclaimed; but she dwelt in illusions—she would have to live and die with Bowdler.

It is difficult to be cursory over this charming woman, who was beautiful without beauty and complete with a dozen deficiencies. The perspective of the stage made her over, and in society she was like the model off the pedestal. She was the picture walking about, which to the artless social mind was a perpetual surprise—a miracle. People thought she told them the secrets of the pictorial nature, in return for which they gave her relaxation and tea. She told them nothing and she drank the tea; but they had, all the same, the best of the bargain. Vawdrey was really at work on a play; but if he had begun it because he liked her I think he let it drag for the same reason. He secretly felt the atrocious difficulty—knew that from his hand the finished piece would have received no active life. At the same time nothing could be more agreeable than to have such a question open with Blanche Adney, and from time to time he put something very good into the play. If he deceived Mrs. Adney it was only because in her despair she was determined to be deceived. To her question about their third act he replied that, before dinner, he had written a magnificent passage.

"Before dinner?" I said. "Why, *cher maître*, before dinner you were holding us all spellbound on the terrace."

My words were a joke, because I thought his had been; but for the first time that I could remember I perceived a certain confusion in his face. He looked at me hard, throwing back his head quickly, the least bit like a horse who has been pulled up short. "Oh, it was before that," he replied, naturally enough.

"Before that you were playing billiards with *me*," Lord Mellifont intimated.

"Then it must have been yesterday," said Vawdrey.

But he was in a tight place. "You told me this morning you did nothing yesterday," the actress objected.

"I don't think I really know when I do things." Vawdrey looked vaguely, without helping himself, at a dish that was offered him.

"It's enough if *we* know," smiled Lord Mellifont.

"I don't believe you've written a line," said Blanche Adney.

"I think I could repeat you the scene." Vawdrey helped himself to *haricots verts*.

"Oh, do—oh, do!" two or three of us cried.

"After dinner, in the salon; it will be an immense *régal*," Lord Mellifont declared.

"I'm not sure, but I'll try," Vawdrey went on.

"Oh, you lovely man!" exclaimed the actress, who was practising Americanisms, being resigned even to an American comedy.

"But there must be this condition," said Vawdrey: "you must make your husband play."

"Play while you're reading? Never!"

"I've too much vanity," said Adney.

Lord Mellifont distinguished him. "You must give us the overture, before the curtain rises. That's a peculiarly delightful moment."

"I sha'n't read—I shall just speak," said Vawdrey.

"Better still, let me go and get your manuscript," the actress suggested.

Vawdrey replied that the manuscript didn't matter; but an hour later, in the salon, we wished he might have had it. We sat expectant, still under the spell of Adney's violin. His wife, in the foreground, on an ottoman, was all impatience and profile, and Lord Mellifont, in the chair—it was always *the* chair, Lord Mellifont's—made our grateful little group feel like a social science congress or a distribution of prizes. Suddenly, instead of beginning, our tame lion began to roar out of tune—he had clean forgotten every word. He was very sorry, but the lines absolutely wouldn't come to him; he was utterly ashamed, but his memory was a blank. He didn't look in the least ashamed—Vawdrey had never looked ashamed in his life; he was only imperturbably and merrily natural. He protested that he had never expected to make such a fool of himself, but we felt that this wouldn't prevent the incident from taking its place among his jolliest reminiscences. It was only *we* who were humiliated, as if he had played us a premeditated trick. This was an occasion, if ever, for Lord Mellifont's tact, which descended on us all like balm: he told us, in his charming artistic way, his way of bridging over arid intervals (he had a *débit*—there was nothing to approach it in England—like the actors of the Comédie Française), of his own collapse on a momentous occasion, the delivery of an address to a mighty multitude, when, finding he had forgotten his memoranda, he fumbled, on the terrible platform, the cynosure of every eye, fumbled vainly in irreproachable pockets for indispensable notes. But the point of his story was finer than that of Vawdrey's pleasantry; for he sketched with a few light gestures the brilliancy of a performance which had risen superior to embarrassment, had resolved itself, we were left to divine, into an effort recognised at the moment as not absolutely a blot on what the public was so good as to call his reputation.

"Play up—play up!" cried Blanche Adney, tapping her husband and remembering how, on the stage, a *contretemps* is always drowned in music. Adney threw himself upon his fiddle, and I said to Clare Vawdrey that his mistake could easily be corrected by his sending for the manuscript. If he would tell me where it was I would immediately fetch it from his room. To this he replied: "My dear fellow, I'm afraid there *is* no manuscript."

"Then you've not written anything?"

"I'll write it to-morrow."

"Ah, you trifle with us," I said, in much mystification.

Vawdrey hesitated an instant. "If there *is* anything, you'll find it on my table."

At this moment one of the others spoke to him, and Lady Mellifont remarked audibly, as if to correct gently our want of consideration, that Mr.

Adney was playing something very beautiful. I had noticed before that she appeared extremely fond of music; she always listened to it in a hushed transport. Vawdrey's attention was drawn away, but it didn't seem to me that the words he had just dropped constituted a definite permission to go to his room. Moreover I wanted to speak to Blanche Adney; I had something to ask her. I had to await my chance, however, as we remained silent awhile for her husband, after which the conversation became general. It was our habit to go to bed early, but there was still a little of the evening left. Before it quite waned I found an opportunity to tell the actress that Vawdrey had given me leave to put my hand on his manuscript. She adjured me, by all I held sacred, to bring it immediately, to give it to her; and her insistence was proof against my suggestion that it would now be too late for him to begin to read: besides which the charm was broken—the others wouldn't care. It was not too late for *her* to begin; therefore I was to possess myself, without more delay, of the precious pages. I told her she should be obeyed in a moment, but I wanted her first to satisfy my just curiosity. What had happened before dinner, while she was on the hills with Lord Mellifont?

"How do you know anything happened?"

"I saw it in your face when you came back."

"And they call me an actress!" cried Mrs. Adney.

"What do they call *me*?" I inquired.

"You're a searcher of hearts—that frivolous thing an observer."

"I wish you'd let an observer write you a play!" I broke out.

"People don't care for what you write: you'd break any run of luck."

"Well, I see plays all round me," I declared; "the air is full of them to-night."

"The air? Thank you for nothing! I only wish my table-drawers were."

"Did he make love to you on the glacier?" I went on.

She stared; then broke into the graduated ecstasy of her laugh. "Lord Mellifont, poor dear? What a funny place! It would indeed be the place for *our* love!"

"Did he fall into a crevasse?" I continued.

Blanche Adney looked at me again as she had done for an instant when she came up, before dinner, with her hands full of flowers. "I don't know into what he fell. I'll tell you to-morrow."

"He did come down, then?"

"Perhaps he went up," she laughed. "It's really strange."

"All the more reason you should tell me to-night."

"I must think it over; I must puzzle it out."

"Oh, if you want conundrums I'll throw in another," I said. "What's the matter with the master?"

"The master of what?"

"Of every form of dissimulation. Vawdrey hasn't written a line."

"Go and get his papers and we'll see."

"I don't like to expose him," I said.

"Why not, if I expose Lord Mellifont?"

"Oh, I'd do anything for that," I conceded. "But why should Vawdrey have made a false statement? It's very curious."

"It's very curious," Blanche Adney repeated, with a musing air and her eyes on Lord Mellifont. Then, rousing herself, she added: "Go and look in his room."

"In Lord Mellifont's?"

She turned to me quickly. "*That* would be a way!"

"A way to what?"

"To find out—to find out!" She spoke gaily and excitedly, but suddenly checked herself. "We're talking nonsense," she said.

"We're mixing things up, but I'm struck with your idea. Get Lady Mellifont to let you."

"Oh, *she* has looked!" Mrs. Adney murmured, with the oddest dramatic expression. Then, after a movement of her beautiful uplifted hand, as if to brush away a fantastic vision, she exclaimed imperiously: "Bring me the scene—bring me the scene!"

"I go for it," I answered; "but don't tell me I can't write a play."

She left me, but my errand was arrested by the approach of a lady who had produced a birthday-book—we had been threatened with it for several evenings—and who did me the honour to solicit my autograph. She had been asking the others, and she couldn't decently leave me out. I could usually remember my name, but it always took me some time to recall my date, and even when I had done so I was never very sure. I hesitated between two days and I remarked to my petitioner that I would sign on both if it would give her any satisfaction. She said that surely I had been born only once; and I replied of course that on the day I made her acquaintance I had been born again. I mention the feeble joke only to show that, with the obligatory inspection of the other autographs, we gave some minutes to this transaction. The lady departed with her book, and then I became aware that the company had dispersed. I was alone in the little salon that had been appropriated to our use. My first impression was one of disappointment: if Vawdrey had gone to bed I didn't wish to disturb him. While I hesitated, however, I recognised that Vawdrey had not gone to bed. A window was open, and the sound of voices outside came in to me: Blanche was on the terrace with her dramatist, and they were talking about the stars. I went to the window for a glimpse—the Alpine night was splendid. My friends had stepped out together; the actress had picked up a cloak; she looked as I had seen her look in the wing of the theatre. They were silent awhile, and I heard the roar of a neighbouring torrent. I turned back into the room, and its quiet lamplight gave me an idea. Our companions had dispersed—it was late for a pastoral country—and we three should have the place to ourselves. Clare Vawdrey had written his scene—it was magnificent; and his reading it to us there, at such an hour, would be an episode intensely memorable. I would bring down his manuscript and meet the two with it as they came in.

I quitted the salon for this purpose; I had been in Vawdrey's room and knew it was on the second floor, the last in a long corridor. A minute later my hand was on the knob of his door, which I naturally pushed open without knocking. It was equally natural that in the absence of its occupant the room should be dark; the more so as, the end of the corridor being at that hour unlighted, the obscurity was not immediately diminished by the opening of the door. I was only aware at first that I had made no mistake and that, the window-curtains not being drawn, I was confronted with a couple of vague starlighted apertures. Their aid, however, was not sufficient to enable me to find what I had come for, and my hand, in my pocket, was already on the little box of matches that I always carried for cigarettes. Suddenly I withdrew it with a start, uttering an ejaculation, an apology. I had entered the wrong room; a glance prolonged for three seconds showed me a figure seated at a table near one of the windows—a figure I had at first taken for a travelling-rug thrown over a chair. I retreated, with a sense of intrusion; but as I did so I became aware, more rapidly than it takes me to express it, in the first place that this was Vawdrey's room and in the second that, most singularly, Vawdrey himself sat before me. Checking myself on the threshold I had a momentary feeling of bewilderment, but before I knew it I had exclaimed: "Hullo! is that you, Vawdrey?"

He neither turned nor answered me, but my question received an immediate and practical reply in the opening of a door on the other side of the passage. A servant, with a candle, had come out of the opposite room, and in this flitting illumination I definitely recognised the man whom, an instant before, I had to the best of my belief left below in conversation with Mrs. Adney. His back was half turned to me, and he bent over the table in the attitude of writing, but I was conscious that I was in no sort of error about his identity. "I beg your pardon—I thought you were downstairs," I said; and as the personage gave no sign of hearing me I added: "If you're busy I won't disturb you." I backed out, closing the door—I had been in the place, I suppose, less than a minute. I had a sense of mystification, which however deepened infinitely the next instant. I stood there with my hand still on the knob of the door, overtaken by the oddest impression of my life. Vawdrey was at his table, writing, and it was a very natural place for him to be; but why was he writing in the dark and why hadn't he answered me? I waited a few seconds for the sound of some movement, to see if he wouldn't rouse himself from his abstraction—a fit conceivable in a great writer—and call out: "Oh, my dear fellow, is it you?" But I heard only the stillness, I felt only the starlighted dusk of the room, with the unexpected presence it enclosed. I turned away, slowly retracing my steps, and came confusedly downstairs. The lamp was still burning in the salon, but the room was empty. I passed round to the door of the hotel and stepped out. Empty too was the terrace. Blanche Adney and the gentleman with her had apparently come in. I hung about five minutes; then I went to bed.

I slept badly, for I was agitated. On looking back at these queer occurrences (you will see presently that they were queer), I perhaps suppose myself more agitated than I was; for great anomalies are never so great at first as after we have reflected upon them. It takes us some time to exhaust explanations. I was vaguely nervous—I had been sharply startled; but there was nothing I could not clear up by asking Blanche Adney, the first thing in the morning, who had been with her on the terrace. Oddly enough, however, when the morning dawned—it dawned admirably—I felt less desire to satisfy myself on this point than to escape, to brush away the shadow of my stupefaction. I saw the day would be splendid, and the fancy took me to spend it, as I had spent happy days of youth, in a lonely mountain ramble. I dressed early, partook of conventional coffee, put a big roll into one pocket and a small flask into the other, and, with a stout stick in my hand, went forth into the high places. My story is not closely concerned with the charming hours I passed there—hours of the kind that make intense memories. If I roamed away half of them on the shoulders of the hills, I lay on the sloping grass for the other half and, with my cap pulled over my eyes (save a peep for immensities of view), listened, in the bright stillness, to the mountain bee and felt most things sink and dwindle.

Clare Vawdrey grew small, Blanche Adney grew dim, Lord Mellifont grew old, and before the day was over I forgot that I had ever been puzzled. When in the late afternoon I made my way down to the inn there was nothing I wanted so much to find out as whether dinner would not soon be ready. To-night I dressed, in a manner, and by the time I was presentable they were all at table.

In their company again my little problem came back to me, so that I was curious to see if Vawdrey wouldn't look at me the least bit queerly. But he didn't look at me at all; which gave me a chance both to be patient and to wonder why I should hesitate to ask him my question across the table. I did hesitate, and with the consciousness of doing so came back a little of the agitation I had left behind me, or below me, during the day. I wasn't ashamed of my scruple, however: it was only a fine discretion. What I vaguely felt was that a public inquiry wouldn't have been fair. Lord Mellifont was there, of course, to mitigate with his perfect manner all consequences; but I think it was present to me that with these particular elements his lordship would not be at home. The moment we got up, therefore, I approached Mrs. Adney, asking her whether, as the evening was lovely, she wouldn't take a turn with me outside.

"You've walked a hundred miles; had you not better be quiet?" she replied.

"I'd walk a hundred miles more to get you to tell me something."

She looked at me an instant, with a little of the queerness that I had sought, but had not found, in Clare Vawdrey's eyes. "Do you mean what became of Lord Mellifont?"

"Of Lord Mellifont?" With my new speculation I had lost that thread.

"Where's your memory, foolish man? We talked of it last evening."

"Ah, yes!" I cried, recalling; "we shall have lots to discuss." I drew her out to the terrace, and before we had gone three steps I said to her: "Who was with you here last night?"

"Last night?" she repeated, as wide of the mark as I had been.

"At ten o'clock—just after our company broke up. You came out here with a gentleman; you talked about the stars."

She stared a moment; then she gave her laugh. "Are you jealous of dear Vawdrey?"

"Then it was he?"

"Certainly it was."

"And how long did he stay?"

"You have it badly. He stayed about a quarter of an hour—perhaps rather more. We walked some distance; he talked about his play. There you have it all; that is the only witchcraft I have used."

"And what did Vawdrey do afterwards?"

"I haven't the least idea. I left him and went to bed."

"At what time did you go to bed?"

"At what time did *you*? I happen to remember that I parted from Mr. Vawdrey at ten twenty-five," said Mrs. Adney. "I came back into the salon to pick up a book, and I noticed the clock."

"In other words you and Vawdrey distinctly lingered here from about five minutes past ten till the hour you mention?"

"I don't know how distinct we were, but we were very jolly. *Où voulez-vous en venir?*" Blanche Adney asked.

"Simply to this, dear lady: that at the time your companion was occupied in the manner you describe, he was also engaged in literary composition in his own room."

She stopped short at this, and her eyes had an expression in the darkness. She wanted to know if I challenged her veracity; and I replied that, on the contrary, I backed it up—it made the case so interesting. She returned that this would only be if she should back up mine; which, however, I had no difficulty in persuading her to do, after I had related to her circumstantially the incident of my quest of the manuscript—the manuscript which, at the time, for a reason I could now understand, appeared to have passed so completely out of her own head.

"His talk made me forget it—I forgot I sent you for it. He made up for his fiasco in the salon: he declaimed me the scene," said my companion. She had dropped on a bench to listen to me and, as we sat there, had briefly cross-examined me. Then she broke out into fresh laughter. "Oh, the eccentricities of genius!"

"They seem greater even than I supposed."

"Oh, the mysteries of greatness!"

"You ought to know all about them, but they take me by surprise."

"Are you absolutely certain it was Mr. Vawdrey?" my companion asked.

"If it wasn't he, who in the world was it? That a strange gentleman, looking exactly like him, should be sitting in his room at that hour of the night and writing at his table *in the dark*," I insisted, "would be practically as wonderful as my own contention."

"Yes, why in the dark?" mused Mrs. Adney.

"Cats can see in the dark," I said.

She smiled at me dimly. "Did it look like a cat?"

"No, dear lady, but I'll tell you what it did look like—it looked like the author of Vawdrey's admirable works. It looked infinitely more like him than our friend does himself," I declared.

"Do you mean it was somebody he gets to do them?"

"Yes, while he dines out and disappoints you."

"Disappoints me?" murmured Mrs. Adney artlessly.

"Disappoints *me*—disappoints every one who looks in him for the genius that created the pages they adore. Where is it in his talk?"

"Ah, last night he was splendid," said the actress.

"He's always splendid, as your morning bath is splendid, or a sirloin of beef, or the railway service to Brighton. But he's never rare."

"I see what you mean."

"That's what makes you such a comfort to talk to. I've often wondered—now I know. There are two of them."

"What a delightful idea!"

"One goes out, the other stays at home. One is the genius, the other's the bourgeois, and it's only the bourgeois whom we personally know. He talks, he circulates, he's awfully popular, he flirts with you—"

"Whereas it's the genius *you* are privileged to see!" Mrs. Adney broke in. "I'm much obliged to you for the distinction."

I laid my hand on her arm. "See him yourself. Try it, test it, go to his room."

"Go to his room? It wouldn't be proper!" she exclaimed, in the tone of her best comedy.

"Anything is proper in such an inquiry. If you see him, it settles it."

"How charming—to settle it!" She thought a moment, then she sprang up. "Do you mean *now*?"

"Whenever you like."

"But suppose I should find the wrong one?" said Blanche Adney, with an exquisite effect.

"The wrong one? Which one do you call the right?"

"The wrong one for a lady to go and see. Suppose I shouldn't find—the genius?"

"Oh, I'll look after the other," I replied. Then, as I had happened to glance about me, I added: "Take care—here comes Lord Mellifont."

"I wish you'd look after *him*," my interlocutress murmured.

"What's the matter with him?"

"That's just what I was going to tell you."

"Tell me now; he's not coming."

Blanche Adney looked a moment. Lord Mellifont, who appeared to have emerged from the hotel to smoke a meditative cigar, had paused, at a distance from us, and stood admiring the wonders of the prospect, discernible even in the dusk. We strolled slowly in another direction, and she presently said: "My idea is almost as droll as yours."

"I don't call mine droll: it's beautiful."

"There's nothing so beautiful as the droll," Mrs. Adney declared.

"You take a professional view. But I'm all ears." My curiosity was indeed alive again.

"Well then, my dear friend, if Clare Vawdrey is double (and I'm bound to say I think that the more of him the better), his lordship there has the opposite complaint: he isn't even whole."

We stopped once more, simultaneously. "I don't understand."

"No more do I. But I have a fancy that if there are two of Mr. Vawdrey, there isn't so much as one, all told, of Lord Mellifont."

I considered a moment, then I laughed out. "I think I see what you mean!"

"That's what makes *you* a comfort. Did you ever see him alone?"

I tried to remember. "Oh, yes; he has been to see me."

"Ah, then he wasn't alone."

"And I've been to see him, in his study."

"Did he know you were there?"

"Naturally—I was announced."

Blanche Adney glanced at me like a lovely conspirator. "You mustn't be announced!" With this she walked on.

I rejoined her, breathless. "Do you mean one must come upon him when he doesn't know it?"

"You must take him unawares. You must go to his room—that's what you must do."

If I was elated by the way our mystery opened out, I was also, pardonably, a little confused. "When I know he's not there?"

"When you know he *is*."

"And what shall I see?"

"You won't see anything!" Mrs. Adney cried as we turned round.

We had reached the end of the terrace, and our movement brought us face to face with Lord Mellifont, who, resuming his walk, had now, without indiscretion, overtaken us. The sight of him at that moment was illuminating, and it kindled a great backward train, connecting itself with one's general impression of the personage. As he stood there smiling at us and waving a practised hand into the transparent night (he introduced the view as if it had been a candidate and "supported" the very Alps), as he rose before us in the delicate fragrance of his cigar and all his other delicacies and fragrances, with more perfections, somehow, heaped upon his handsome head than one had ever seen accumulated before, he struck me as so essentially, so conspicuously and uniformly the public character that I read in a flash the answer to Blanche Adney's riddle. He was all public and had no corresponding private life, just as Clare Vawdrey was all private and had no corresponding public one. I had heard only half my companion's story, yet as we joined Lord Mellifont (he had followed us—he liked Mrs. Adney; but it was always to be conceived of him that he accepted society rather than sought it), as we participated for half an hour in the distributed wealth of his conversation, I felt with unabashed duplicity that we had, as it were, found him out. I was even more deeply diverted by that whisk of the curtain to which the actress had just treated me than I had been by my own discovery; and if I was not ashamed of my share of her secret any more than of having divided my own with her (though my own was, of the two mysteries, the more glorious for the personage involved), this was because there was no cruelty in my advantage, but on the contrary an extreme tenderness and a positive compassion. Oh, he was safe with me, and I felt moreover rich and enlightened, as if I had suddenly put the universe into my pocket. I had learned what an affair of the spot and the moment a great appearance may be. It would doubtless be too much to say that I had always suspected the possibility, in the background of his lordship's being, of some such beautiful instance; but it is at least a fact that, patronising as it sounds, I had been conscious of a certain reserve of indulgence for him. I had secretly pitied him for the perfection of his performance, had wondered what blank face such a mask had to cover, what was left to him for the immitigable hours in which a man sits down with himself, or, more serious still, with that intenser self, his lawful wife. How was he at home and what did he do when he was alone? There was something in Lady Mellifont that gave a point to these researches—something that suggested that even to her he was still the public character and that she was haunted by similar questionings. She had never cleared them up: that was her eternal trouble. We therefore knew more than she did, Blanche Adney and I; but we wouldn't tell her for the world, nor would she probably thank us for doing so. She preferred the relative grandeur of uncertainty. She was not at home with him, so she couldn't say; and with her he was not alone, so he couldn't show her. He represented to his wife and he was a hero to his servants, and what one wanted to arrive at was what really became of him when no eye could see. He rested, presumably; but what form of rest could repair such a plenitude of presence? Lady Mellifont was too proud to pry, and as she had never looked through a keyhole she remained dignified and unassuaged.

It may have been a fancy of mine that Blanche Adney drew out our companion, or it may be that the practical irony of our relation to him at such a moment made me see him more vividly: at any rate he never had struck me as so dissimilar from what he would have been if we had not offered him a reflection of his image. We were only a concourse of two, but he had never been more public. His perfect manner had never been more perfect, his remarkable tact had never been more remarkable. I had a tacit sense that it would all be in the morning papers, with a leader, and also a secretly exhilarating one that I knew something that wouldn't be, that never could be, though any enterprising journal would give one a fortune for it. I must add, however, that in spite of my enjoyment—it was almost sensual, like that of a consummate dish—I was eager to be alone again with Mrs. Adney, who owed me an anecdote. It proved impossible, that evening, for some of the others came out to see what we found so absorbing; and then Lord Mellifont bespoke a little music from the fiddler, who produced his violin and played to us divinely, on our platform of echoes, face to face with the ghosts of the mountains. Before the concert was over I missed our actress and, glancing into the window of the salon, saw that she was established with Vawdrey, who was reading to her from a manuscript. The great scene had apparently been achieved and was doubtless the more interesting to Blanche from the new lights she had gathered about its author. I judged it discreet not to disturb them, and I went to bed without seeing her again. I looked out for her betimes the next morning and, as the promise of the day was fair, proposed to her that we should take to the hills, reminding her of the high obligation she had incurred. She recognised the obligation and gratified me with her company; but before we had strolled ten yards up the pass she broke out with intensity: "My dear friend, you've no idea how it works in me! I can think of nothing else."

"Than your theory about Lord Mellifont?"

"Oh, bother Lord Mellifont! I allude to yours about Mr. Vawdrey, who is much the more interesting person of the two. I'm fascinated by that vision of his—what-do-you-call-it?"

"His alternative identity?"

"His other self: that's easier to say."

"You accept it, then, you adopt it?"

"Adopt it? I rejoice in it! It became tremendously vivid to me last evening."

"While he read to you there?"

"Yes, as I listened to him, watched him. It simplified everything, explained everything."

"That's indeed the blessing of it. Is the scene very fine?"

"Magnificent, and he reads beautifully."

"Almost as well as the other one writes!" I laughed.

This made my companion stop a moment, laying her hand on my arm. "You utter my very impression. I felt that he was reading me the work of another man."

"What a service to the other man!"

"Such a totally different person," said Mrs. Adney. We talked of this difference as we went on, and of what a wealth it constituted, what a resource for life, such a duplication of character.

"It ought to make him live twice as long as other people," I observed.

"Ought to make which of them?"

"Well, both; for after all they're members of a firm, and one of them couldn't carry on the business without the other. Moreover mere survival would be dreadful for either."

Blanche Adney was silent a little; then she exclaimed: "I don't know—I wish he *would* survive!"

"May I, on my side, inquire which?"

"If you can't guess I won't tell you."

"I know the heart of woman. You always prefer the other."

She halted again, looking round her. "Off here, away from my husband, I *can* tell you. I'm in love with him!"

"Unhappy woman, he has no passions," I answered.

"That's exactly why I adore him. Doesn't a woman with my history know that the passions of others are insupportable? An actress, poor thing, can't care for any love that's not all on *her* side; she can't afford to be repaid. My marriage proves that: marriage is ruinous. Do you know what was in my mind last night, all the while Mr. Vawdrey was reading me those beautiful speeches? An insane desire to see the author." And dramatically, as if to hide her shame, Blanche Adney passed on.

"We'll manage that," I returned. "I want another glimpse of him myself. But meanwhile please remember that I've been waiting more than forty-eight hours for the evidence that supports your sketch, intensely suggestive and plausible, of Lord Mellifont's private life."

"Oh, Lord Mellifont doesn't interest me."

"He did yesterday," I said.

"Yes, but that was before I fell in love. You blotted him out with your story."

"You'll make me sorry I told it. Come," I pleaded, "if you don't let me know how your idea came into your head I shall imagine you simply made it up."

"Let me recollect then, while we wander in this grassy valley."

We stood at the entrance of a charming crooked gorge, a portion of whose level floor formed the bed of a stream that was smooth with swiftness. We turned into it, and the soft walk beside the clear torrent drew us on and on; till suddenly, as we continued and I waited for my companion to remember, a bend of the valley showed us Lady Mellifont coming toward us. She was alone, under the canopy of her parasol, drawing her sable train over the turf; and in this form, on the devious ways, she was a sufficiently rare apparition. She usually took a footman, who marched behind her on the highroads and whose livery was strange to the mountaineers. She blushed on seeing us, as if she ought somehow to justify herself; she laughed vaguely and said she had come out for a little early stroll. We stood together a moment, exchanging platitudes, and then she remarked that she had thought she might find her husband.

"Is he in this quarter?" I inquired.

"I supposed he would be. He came out an hour ago to sketch."

"Have you been looking for him?" Mrs. Adney asked.

"A little; not very much," said Lady Mellifont.

Each of the women rested her eyes with some intensity, as it seemed to me, on the eyes of the other.

"We'll look for him *for* you, if you like," said Mrs. Adney.

"Oh, it doesn't matter. I thought I'd join him."

"He won't make his sketch if you don't," my companion hinted.

"Perhaps he will if *you* do," said Lady Mellifont.

"Oh, I dare say he'll turn up," I interposed.

"He certainly will if he knows we're here!" Blanche Adney retorted.

"Will you wait while we search?" I asked of Lady Mellifont.

She repeated that it was of no consequence; upon which Mrs. Adney went on: "We'll go into the matter for our own pleasure."

"I wish you a pleasant expedition," said her ladyship, and was turning away when I sought to know if we should inform her husband that she had followed him. She hesitated a moment; then she jerked out oddly: "I think you had better not." With this she took leave of us, floating a little stiffly down the gorge.

My companion and I watched her retreat, then we exchanged a stare, while a light ghost of a laugh rippled from the actress's lips. "She might be walking in the shrubberies at Mellifont!"

"She suspects it, you know," I replied.

"And she doesn't want him to know it. There won't be any sketch."

"Unless we overtake him," I subjoined. "In that case we shall find him producing one, in the most graceful attitude, and the queer thing is that it will be brilliant."

"Let us leave him alone—he'll have to come home without it."

"He'd rather never come home. Oh, he'll find a public!"

"Perhaps he'll do it for the cows," Blanche Adney suggested; and as I was on the point of rebuking her profanity she went on: "That's simply what I happened to discover."

"What are you speaking of?"

"The incident of day before yesterday."

"Ah, let's have it at last!"

"That's all it was—that I was like Lady Mellifont: I couldn't find him."

"Did you lose him?"

"He lost *me*—that appears to be the way of it. He thought I was gone."

"But you did find him, since you came home with him."

"It was he who found *me*. That again is what must happen. He's there from the moment he knows somebody else is."

"I understand his intermissions," I said after a short reflection, "but I don't quite seize the law that governs them."

"Oh, it's a fine shade, but I caught it at that moment. I had started to come home. I was tired, and I had insisted on his not coming back with me. We had found some rare flowers—those I brought home—and it was he who had discovered almost all of them. It amused him very much, and I knew he wanted to get more; but I was weary and I quitted him. He let me go—where else would have been his tact?—and I was too stupid then to have guessed that from the moment I was not there no flower would be gathered. I started homeward, but at the end of three minutes I found I had brought away his penknife—he had lent it to me to trim a branch—and I knew he would need it. I turned back a few steps, to call him, but before I spoke I looked about for him. You can't understand what happened then without having the place before you."

"You must take me there," I said.

"We may see the wonder here. The place was simply one that offered no chance for concealment—a great gradual hillside, without obstructions or trees. There were some rocks below me, behind which I myself had disappeared, but from which on coming back I immediately emerged again."

"Then he must have seen you."

"He was too utterly gone, for some reason best known to himself. It was probably some moment of fatigue—he's getting on, you know, so that, with the sense of returning solitude, the reaction had been proportionately great, the extinction proportionately complete. At any rate the stage was as bare as your hand."

"Could he have been somewhere else?"

"He couldn't have been, in the time, anywhere but where I had left him. Yet the place was utterly empty—as empty as this stretch of valley before us. He had vanished—he had ceased to be. But as soon as my voice rang out (I uttered his name), he rose before me like the rising sun."

"And where did the sun rise?"

"Just where it ought to—just where he would have been and where I should have seen him had he been like other people."

I had listened with the deepest interest, but it was my duty to think of objections. "How long a time elapsed between the moment you perceived his absence and the moment you called?"

"Oh, only an instant. I don't pretend it was long."

"Long enough for you to be sure?" I said.

"Sure he wasn't there?"

"Yes, and that you were not mistaken, not the victim of some hocus-pocus of your eyesight."

"I may have been mistaken, but I don't believe it. At any rate, that's just why I want you to look in his room."

I thought a moment. "How *can* I, when even his wife doesn't dare to?"

"She *wants* to; propose it to her. It wouldn't take much to make her. She does suspect."

I thought another moment. "Did he seem to know?"

"That I had missed him? So it struck me, but he thought he had been quick enough."

"Did you speak of his disappearance?"

"Heaven forbid! It seemed to me too strange."

"Quite right. And how did he look?"

Trying to think it out again and reconstitute her miracle, Blanche Adney gazed abstractedly up the valley. Suddenly she exclaimed: "Just as he looks now!" and I saw Lord Mellifont stand before us with his sketch-block. I perceived, as we met him, that he looked neither suspicious nor blank: he looked simply, as he did always, everywhere, the principal feature of the scene. Naturally he had no sketch to show us, but nothing could better have rounded off our actual conception of him than the way he fell into position as we approached. He had been selecting his point of view; he took possession of it with a flourish of the pencil. He leaned against a rock;

his beautiful little box of water-colours reposed on a natural table beside him, a ledge of the bank which showed how inveterately nature ministered to his convenience. He painted while he talked and he talked while he painted; and if the painting was as miscellaneous as the talk, the talk would equally have graced an album. We waited while the exhibition went on, and it seemed indeed as if the conscious profiles of the peaks were interested in his success. They grew as black as silhouettes in paper, sharp against a livid sky from which, however, there would be nothing to fear till Lord Mellifont's sketch should be finished. Blanche Adney communed with me dumbly, and I could read the language of her eyes: "Oh, if *we* could only do it as well as that! He fills the stage in a way that beats us." We could no more have left him than we could have quitted the theatre till the play was over; but in due time we turned round with him and strolled back to the inn, before the door of which his lordship, glancing again at his picture, tore the fresh leaf from the block and presented it with a few happy words to Mrs. Adney. Then he went into the house; and a moment later, looking up from where we stood, we saw him, above, at the window of his sitting-room (he had the best apartments), watching the signs of the weather.

"He'll have to rest after this," Blanche said, dropping her eyes on her water-colour.

"Indeed he will!" I raised mine to the window: Lord Mellifont had vanished. "He's already reabsorbed."

"Reabsorbed?" I could see the actress was now thinking of something else.

"Into the immensity of things. He has lapsed again; there's an *entr'acte*."

"It ought to be long." Mrs. Adney looked up and down the terrace, and at that moment the head-waiter appeared in the doorway. Suddenly she turned to this functionary with the question: "Have you seen Mr. Vawdrey lately?"

The man immediately approached. "He left the house five minutes ago—for a walk, I think. He went down the pass; he had a book."

I was watching the ominous clouds. "He had better have had an umbrella."

The waiter smiled. "I recommended him to take one."

"Thank you," said Mrs. Adney; and the Oberkellner withdrew. Then she went on, abruptly: "Will you do me a favour?"

"Yes, if you'll do *me* one. Let me see if your picture is signed."

She glanced at the sketch before giving it to me. "For a wonder it isn't."

"It ought to be, for full value. May I keep it awhile?"

"Yes, if you'll do what I ask. Take an umbrella and go after Mr. Vawdrey."

"To bring him to Mrs. Adney?"

"To keep him out—as long as you can."

"I'll keep him as long as the rain holds off."

"Oh, never mind the rain!" my companion exclaimed.

"Would you have us drenched?"

"Without remorse." Then with a strange light in her eyes she added: "I'm going to try."

"To try?"

"To see the real one. Oh, if I can get at him!" she broke out with passion.

"Try, try!" I replied. "I'll keep our friend all day."

"If I can get at the one who does it"—and she paused, with shining eyes—"if I can have it out with him I shall get my part!"

"I'll keep Vawdrey for ever!" I called after her as she passed quickly into the house.

Her audacity was communicative, and I stood there in a glow of excitement. I looked at Lord Mellifont's water-colour and I looked at the gathering storm; I turned my eyes again to his lordship's windows and then I bent them on my watch. Vawdrey had so little the start of me that I should have time to overtake him—time even if I should take five minutes to go up to Lord Mellifont's sitting-room (where we had all been hospitably received), and say to him, as a messenger, that Mrs. Adney begged he would bestow upon his sketch the high consecration of his signature. As I again considered this work of art I perceived there was something it certainly did lack: what else then but so noble an autograph? It was my duty to supply the deficiency without delay, and in accordance with this conviction I instantly re-entered the hotel. I went up to Lord Mellifont's apartments; I reached the door of his salon. Here, however, I was met by a difficulty of which my extravagance had not taken account. If I were to knock I should spoil everything; yet was I prepared to dispense with this ceremony? I asked myself the question, and it embarrassed me; I turned my little picture round and round, but it didn't give me the answer I wanted. I wanted it to say: "Open the door gently, gently, without a sound, yet very quickly: then you will see what you will see." I had gone so far as to lay my hand, upon the knob when I became aware (having my wits so about me), that exactly in the manner I was thinking of—gently, gently, without a sound—another door had moved, on the opposite side of the hall. At the same instant I found myself smiling rather constrainedly upon Lady Mellifont, who, on seeing me, had checked herself on the threshold of her room. For a moment, as she stood there, we exchanged two or three ideas that were the more singular for being unspoken. We had caught each other hovering, and we understood each other; but as I stepped over to her (so that we were separated from the sitting-room by the width of the hall), her lips formed the almost soundless entreaty: "Don't!" I could see in her conscious eyes everything that the word expressed—the confession of her own curiosity and the dread of the consequences of mine. "*Don't!*" she repeated, as I stood before her. From the moment my experiment could strike her as an act of violence I was ready to renounce it; yet I thought I detected in her frightened face a still deeper betrayal—a possibility of disappointment if I should give way. It was as if she had said: "I'll let you do it if you'll take the responsibility. Yes, with some one else I'd surprise him. But it would never do for him to think it was I."

"We soon found Lord Mellifont," I observed, in allusion to our encounter with her an hour before, "and he was so good as to give this lovely sketch to Mrs. Adney, who has asked me to come up and beg him to put in the omitted signature."

Lady Mellifont took the drawing from me, and I could guess the struggle that went on in her while she looked at it. She was silent for some time; then I felt that all her delicacies and dignities, all her old timidities and pieties were fighting against her opportunity. She turned away from me and, with the drawing, went back to her room. She was absent for a couple of minutes, and when she reappeared I could see that she had vanquished her temptation; that even, with a kind of resurgent horror, she had shrunk from it. She had deposited the sketch in the room. "If you will kindly leave the picture with me, I will see that Mrs. Adney's request is attended to," she said, with great courtesy and sweetness, but in a manner that put an end to our colloquy.

I assented, with a somewhat artificial enthusiasm perhaps, and then, to ease off our separation, remarked that we were going to have a change of weather.

"In that case we shall go—we shall go immediately," said Lady Mellifont. I was amused at the eagerness with which she made this declaration: it appeared to represent a coveted flight into safety, an escape with her threatened secret. I was the more surprised therefore when, as I was turning away, she put out her hand to take mine. She had the pretext of bidding me farewell, but as I shook hands with her on this supposition I felt that what the movement really conveyed was: "I thank you for the help you would have given me, but it's better as it is. If I should know, who would help me then?" As I went to my room to get my umbrella I said to myself: "She's sure, but she won't put it to the proof."

A quarter of an hour later I had overtaken Clare Vawdrey in the pass, and shortly after this we found ourselves looking for refuge. The storm had not only completely gathered, but it had broken at the last with extraordinary rapidity. We scrambled up a hillside to an empty cabin, a rough structure that was hardly more than a shed for the protection of cattle. It was a tolerable shelter however, and it had fissures through which we could watch the splendid spectacle of the tempest. This entertainment lasted an hour—an hour that has remained with me as full of odd disparities. While the lightning played with the thunder and the rain gushed in on our umbrellas, I said to myself that Clare Vawdrey was disappointing. I don't know exactly what I should have predicated of a great author exposed to the fury of the elements, I can't say what particular Manfred attitude I should have expected my companion to assume, but it seemed to me somehow that I shouldn't have looked to him to regale me in such a situation with stories (which I had already heard), about the celebrated Lady Ringrose. Her ladyship formed the subject of Vawdrey's conversation during this prodigious scene, though before it was quite over he had launched out on Mr. Chafer, the scarcely less notorious reviewer. It broke my heart to hear a man like Vawdrey talk of reviewers. The lightning projected a hard clearness upon the truth, familiar to me for years, to which the last day or two had added transcendent support—the irritating certitude that for personal relations this admirable genius thought his second-best good enough. It was, no doubt, as society was made, but there was a contempt in the distinction which could not fail to be galling to an admirer. The world was vulgar and stupid, and the real man would have been a fool to come out for it when he could gossip and dine by deputy. None the less my heart sank as I felt my companion practice this economy. I don't know exactly what I wanted; I suppose I wanted him to make an exception for *me*. I almost believed he would, if he had known how I worshipped his talent. But I had never been able to translate this to him, and his application of his principle was relentless. At any rate I was more than ever sure that at such an hour his chair at home was not empty: *there* was the Manfred attitude, *there* were the responsive flashes. I could only envy Mrs. Adney her presumable enjoyment of them.

The weather drew off at last, and the rain abated sufficiently to allow us to emerge from our asylum and make our way back to the inn, where we found on our arrival that our prolonged absence had produced some agitation. It was judged apparently that the fury of the elements might have placed us in a predicament. Several of our friends were at the door, and they seemed a little disconcerted when it was perceived that we were only drenched. Clare Vawdrey, for some reason, was wetter than I, and he took his course to his room. Blanche Adney was among the persons collected to look out for us, but as Vawdrey came toward her she shrank from him, without a greeting; with a movement that I observed as almost one of estrangement she turned her back on him and went quickly into the salon. Wet as I was I went in after her; on which she immediately flung round and faced me. The first thing I saw was that she had never been so beautiful. There was a light of inspiration in her face, and she broke out to me in the quickest whisper, which was at the same time the loudest cry, I have ever heard: "I've got my *part!*"

"You went to his room—I was right?"

"Right?" Blanche Adney repeated. "Ah, my dear fellow!" she murmured.

"He was there—you saw him?"

"He saw me. It was the hour of my life!"

"It must have been the hour of his, if you were half as lovely as you are at this moment."

"He's splendid," she pursued, as if she didn't hear me. "He *is* the one who does it!" I listened, immensely impressed, and she added: "We understood each other."

"By flashes of lightning?"

"Oh, I didn't see the lightning then!"

"How long were you there?" I asked with admiration.

"Long enough to tell him I adore him."

"Ah, that's what I've never been able to tell him!" I exclaimed ruefully.

"I shall have my part—I shall have my part!" she continued, with triumphant indifference; and she flung round the room with the joy of a girl, only checking herself to say: "Go and change your clothes."

"You shall have Lord Mellifont's signature," I said.

"Oh, bother Lord Mellifont's signature! He's far nicer than Mr. Vawdrey," she went on irrelevantly.

"Lord Mellifont?" I pretended to inquire.

"Confound Lord Mellifont!" And Blanche Adney, in her elation, brushed by me, whisking again through the open door. Just outside of it she came upon her husband; whereupon, with a charming cry of "We're talking of you, my love!" she threw herself upon him and kissed him.

I went to my room and changed my clothes, but I remained there till the evening. The violence of the storm had passed over us, but the rain had settled down to a drizzle. On descending to dinner I found that the change in the weather had already broken up our party. The Mellifonts had departed in a carriage and four, they had been followed by others, and several vehicles had been bespoken for the morning. Blanche Adney's was one of them, and on the pretext that she had preparations to make she quitted us directly after dinner. Clare Vawdrey asked me what was the matter with her—she suddenly appeared to dislike him. I forget what answer I gave, but I did my best to comfort him by driving away with him the next day. Mrs. Adney had vanished when we came down; but they made up their quarrel in London, for he finished his play, which she produced. I must add that she is still, nevertheless, in want of the great part. I have a beautiful one in my head, but she doesn't come to see me to stir me up about it. Lady Mellifont always drops me a kind word when we meet, but that doesn't console me.

THE WHEEL OF TIME

I

"And your daughter?" said Lady Greyswood; "tell me about her. She must be nice."

"Oh, yes, she's nice enough. She's a great comfort."

Mrs. Knocker hesitated a moment, then she went on: "Unfortunately she's not good-looking—not a bit."

"That doesn't matter, when they're not ill-natured," rejoined, insincerely, Lady Greyswood, who had the remains of great beauty.

"Oh, but poor Fanny is quite extraordinarily plain. I assure you it does matter. She knows it herself; she suffers from it. It's the sort of thing that makes a great difference in a girl's life."

"But if she's charming, if she's clever!" said Lady Greyswood, with more benevolence than logic. "I've known plain women who were liked."

"Do you mean *me*, my dear?" her old friend straightforwardly inquired. "But I'm not so awfully liked!"

"You?" Lady Greyswood exclaimed. "Why, you're grand!"

"I'm not so repulsive as I was when I was young perhaps, but that's not saying much."

"As when you were young!" laughed Lady Greyswood. "You sweet thing, you *are* young. I thought India dried people up."

"Oh, when you're a mummy to begin with!" Mrs. Knocker returned, with her trick of self-abasement. "Of course I've not been such a fool as to keep my children there. My girl *is* clever," she continued, "but she's afraid to show it. Therefore you may judge whether, with her unfortunate appearance, she's charming."

"She shall show it to *me!* You must let me do everything for her."

"Does that include finding her a husband? I should like her to show it to someone who'll marry her."

"*I*'ll marry her!" said Lady Greyswood, who was handsomer than ever when she laughed and looked capable.

"What a blessing to meet you this way on the threshold of home! I give you notice that I shall cling to you. But that's what I meant; that's the thing the want of beauty makes so difficult—as if it were not difficult enough at the best."

"My dear child, one meets plenty of ugly women with husbands," Lady Greyswood argued, "and often with very nice ones."

"Yes, mine is very nice. There are men who don't mind one's face, for whom beauty isn't indispensable, but they are rare. I don't understand them. If I'd been a man about to marry I should have gone in for looks. However, the poor child will *have* something," Mrs. Knocker continued.

Lady Greyswood rested thoughtful eyes on her. "Do you mean she'll be well off?"

"We shall do everything we can for her. We're not in such misery as we used to be. We've managed to save in India, strange to say, and six months ago my husband came into money (more than we had ever dreamed of), by the death of his poor brother. We feel quite opulent (it's rather nice!) and we should expect to do something decent for our daughter. I don't mind it's being known."

"It *shall* be known!" said Lady Greyswood, getting up. "Leave the dear child to me!" The old friends embraced, for the porter of the hotel had come in to say that the carriage ordered for her ladyship was at the door. They had met in Paris by the merest chance, in the court of an inn, after a separation of years, just as Lady Greyswood was going home. She had been to Aix-les-Bains early in the season and was resting on her way back to England. Mrs. Knocker and the General, bringing their eastern exile to a close, had arrived only the night before from Marseilles and were to wait in Paris for their children, a tall girl and two younger boys, who, inevitably dissociated from their parents, had been for the past two years with a devoted aunt, their father's maiden sister, at Heidelberg. The reunion of the family was to take place with jollity in Paris, whither this good lady was now hurrying with her drilled and demoralized charges. Mrs. Knocker had come to England to see them two years before, and the period at Heidelberg had been planned during this visit. With the termination of her husband's service a new life opened before them all, and they had plans of comprehensive rejoicing for the summer—plans involving however a continuance, for a few months, of useful foreign opportunities, during which various questions connected with the organization of a final home in England were practically to be dealt with. There was to be a salubrious house on the continent, taken in some neighbourhood that would both yield a stimulus to plain Fanny's French (her German was much commended), and permit of frequent "running over" for the General. With these preoccupations Mrs. Knocker, after her delightful encounter with Lady Greyswood, was less keenly conscious of the variations of destiny than she had been when, at the age of twenty, that intimate friend of her youth, beautiful, loveable and about to be united to a nobleman of ancient name, was brightly, almost insolently alienated. The less attractive of the two girls had married only several years later, and her marriage had perhaps emphasised the divergence of their ways. To-day however the inequality, as Mrs. Knocker would have phrased it, rather dropped out of the impression produced by the somewhat wasted and faded dowager, exquisite still, but unexpectedly appealing, who made no secret (an attempt that in an age of such publicity would have been useless), of what she had had, in vulgar parlance, to put up with, or of her having been left badly off. She had spoken of her children—she had had no less than six—but she had evidently thought it better not to speak of her husband. That somehow made up, on Mrs. Knocker's part, for some ancient aches.

It was not till a year after this incident that, one day in London, in her little house in Queen Street, Lady Greyswood said to her third son, Maurice—the one she was fondest of, the one who on his own side had given her most signs of affection:

"I don't see what there is for you but to marry a girl of a certain fortune."

"Oh, that's not my line! I may be an idiot, but I'm not mercenary," the young man declared. He was not an idiot, but there was an examination, rather stiff indeed, to which, without success, he had gone up twice. The diplomatic service was closed to him by this catastrophe; nothing else appeared particularly open; he was terribly at leisure. There had been a theory none the less that he was the ablest of the family. Two of his brothers had been squeezed into the army and had declared rather crudely that they would do their best to keep Maurice out. They were not put to any trouble in this respect however, as he professed a complete indifference to the trade of arms. His mother, who was vague about everything except the idea that people ought to like him, if only for his extraordinary good looks, thought it strange there shouldn't be some opening for him in political life, or something to be picked up even in the City. But no bustling borough solicited the advantage of his protection, no eminent statesman in want of a secretary took him by the hand, no great commercial house had been keeping a stool for him. Maurice, in a word, was not "approached" from any quarter, and meanwhile he was as irritating as the intending traveller who allows you the pleasure of looking out his railway-connections. Poor Lady Greyswood fumbled the social Bradshaw in vain. The young man had only one marked taste, with which his mother saw no way to deal—an invincible passion for photography. He was perpetually taking shots at his friends, but she couldn't open premises for him in Baker Street. He smoked endless cigarettes—she was sure they made him languid. She would have been more displeased with him if she had not felt so vividly that someone ought to do something for him; nevertheless she almost lost patience at his remark about not being mercenary. She was on the point of asking him what he called it to live on his relations, but she checked the words as she remembered that she herself was the only one who did much for him. Nevertheless, as she hated open professions of disinterestedness, she replied that that was a nonsensical tone. Whatever one should get in such a way one would give quite as much, even if it didn't happen to be money; and when he inquired in return what it was (beyond the disgrace of his failures) that she judged a fellow like him would bring to his bride, she replied that he would bring himself, his personal qualities (she didn't like to be more definite about his appearance), his name, his descent, his connections—good honest commodities all, for which any girl of proper feeling would be glad to pay. Such a name as that of the Glanvils was surely worth something, and she appealed to him to try what he could do with it.

"Surely I can do something better with it than sell it," said Maurice.

"I should like then very much to hear what," she replied very calmly, waiting reasonably for his answer. She waited to no purpose; the question baffled him, like those of his examinations. She explained that she meant of course that he should care for the girl, who might easily have a worse fault than the command of bread and butter. To humour her, for he was always good-natured, he said after a moment, smiling:

"Dear mother, is she pretty?"

"Is who pretty?"

"The young lady you have in your eye. Of course I see you've picked her out."

She coloured slightly at this—she had planned a more gradual revelation. For an instant she thought of saying that she had only had a general idea, for the form of his question embarrassed her; but on reflection she determined to be frank and practical. "Well, I confess I *am* thinking of a girl—a very nice one. But she hasn't great beauty."

"Oh, then it's of no use."

"But she's delightful, and she'll have thirty thousand pounds down, to say nothing of expectations."

Maurice Glanvil looked at his mother. "She must be hideous—for you to admit it. Therefore if she's rich she becomes quite impossible; for how can a fellow have the air of having been bribed with gold to marry a monster?"

"Fanny Knocker isn't the least a monster, and I can see that she'll improve. She's tall, and she's quite strong, and there's nothing at all disagreeable about her. Remember that you can't have everything."

"I thought you contended that I could!" said Maurice, amused at his mother's description of her young friend's charms. He had never heard anyone damned, as regards that sort of thing, with fainter praise. He declared that he would be perfectly capable of marrying a poor girl, but that the prime necessity in any young person he should think of would be the possession of a face—to put it at the least—that it would give him positive pleasure to look at. "I don't ask for much, but I do ask for beauty," he went on. "My eye must be gratified—I must have a wife I can photograph."

Lady Greyswood was tempted to answer that he himself had good looks enough to make a handsome couple, but she withheld the remark as injudicious, though effective, for it was a part of her son's amiability that he appeared to have no conception of his plastic side. He would have been disgusted if she had put it forward; if he had the ideal he had just described it was not because his own profile was his standard. What she herself saw in it was a force for coercing heiresses. She had however to be patient, and she promised herself to be adroit; which was all the easier as she really liked Fanny Knocker.

The girl's parents had at last taken a house in Ennismore Gardens, and the friend of her mother's youth had been confronted with the question of redeeming the pledges uttered in Paris. This unsophisticated and united family, with relations to visit and schoolboys' holidays to outlive, had spent the winter in the country and had but lately begun to talk of itself, extravagantly of course, through Mrs. Knocker's droll lips, as open to social attentions. Lady Greyswood had not been false to her vows; she had on the contrary recognised from the first that, if he could only be made to see it, Fanny Knocker would be just the person to fill out poor Maurice's blanks. She had kept this confidence to herself, but it had made her very kind to the young lady. One of the forms of this kindness had been an ingenuity in keeping her from coming to Queen Street until Maurice should have been prepared. Was he to be regarded as prepared now that he asserted he would have nothing to do with Miss Knocker? This was a question that worried Lady Greyswood, who at any rate said to herself that she had told him the worst. Her idea had been to sound her old friend only after the young people should have met and Fanny should have fallen in love. Such a catastrophe for Fanny belonged for Lady Greyswood to that order of convenience that she could always take for granted.

She had found the girl, as she expected, ugly and awkward, but had also discovered a charm of character in her intelligent timidity. No one knew better than this observant woman how thankless a task in general it was in London to "take out" a plain girl; she had seen the nicest creatures, in the brutality of balls, participate only through wistful, almost tearful eyes; her little drawing-room, at intimate hours, had been shaken by the confidences of desperate mothers. None the less she felt sure that Fanny's path would not be rugged; thirty thousand pounds were a fine set of features, and her anxiety was rather on the score of the expectations of the young lady's parents. Mrs. Knocker had dropped remarks suggestive of a high imagination, of the conviction that there might be a real efficacy in what they were doing for their daughter. The danger, in other words, might well be that no younger son need apply—a possibility that made Lady Greyswood take all her precautions. The acceptability of her favourite child was consistent with the rejection of those of other people—on which indeed it even directly depended. She remembered on the other hand the proverb about taking your horse to the water; the crystalline spring of her young friend's homage might overflow, but she couldn't compel her boy to drink. The clever way was to break down his prejudice—to get him to consent to give poor Fanny a chance. Therefore if she was careful not to worry him she let him see her project as something patient and deeply wise; she had the air of waiting resignedly for the day on which, in the absence of other solutions, he would say to her: "Well, let me have a look at my fate!" Meanwhile moreover she was nothing if not conscientious, and as she had made up her mind about the girl's susceptibility she had a scruple against exposing her. This exposure would not be justified so long as Maurice's theoretic rigour should remain unabated.

She felt virtuous in carrying her scruple to the point of rudeness; she knew that Jane Knocker wondered why, though so attentive in a hundred ways, she had never definitely included the poor child in any invitation to Queen Street. There came a moment when it gave her pleasure to suspect that her old friend had begun to explain this omission by the idea of a positive exaggeration of good faith—an honest recognition of the detrimental character of the young man in ambush there. As Maurice, though much addicted to kissing his mother at home, never dangled about her in public, he had remained a mythical figure to Mrs. Knocker: he had been absent (culpably—there was a touch of the inevitable incivility in it), on each of the occasions on which, after their arrival in London, she and her husband dined with Lady Greyswood. This astute woman knew that her delightful Jane was whimsical enough to be excited good-humouredly by a mystery: she might very well want to make Maurice's acquaintance in just the degree in which she guessed that his mother's high sense of honour kept him out of the way. Moreover she desired intensely that her daughter should have the sort of experience that would help her to take confidence. Lady Greyswood knew that no one had as yet asked the girl to dinner and that this particular attention was the one for which her mother would be most grateful. No sooner had she arrived at these illuminations than, with deep diplomacy, she requested the pleasure of the company of her dear Jane and the General. Mrs. Knocker accepted with delight—she always accepted with delight—so that nothing remained for Lady Greyswood but to make sure of Maurice in advance. After this was done she had only to wait. When the dinner, on a day very near at hand, took place (she had jumped at the first evening on which the Knockers were free), she had the gratification of seeing her prevision exactly fulfilled. Her whimsical Jane had thrown the game into her hands, had been taken at the very last moment with one of her Indian headaches and, infinitely apologetic and explanatory, had hustled poor Fanny off with the General. The girl, flurried and frightened by her responsibility, sat at dinner next to Maurice, who behaved beautifully—not in the least as the victim of a trick; and when a fortnight later Lady Greyswood was able to divine that her mind from that evening had been filled with a virginal ecstasy, she was also fortunately able to feel serenely, delightfully guiltless.

II

She knew this fact about Fanny's mind, she believed, some time before Jane Knocker knew it; but she also had reason to think that Jane Knocker had known it for some time before she spoke of it. It was not till the middle of June, after a succession of encounters between the young people, that her old friend came one morning to discuss the circumstance. Mrs. Knocker asked her if she suspected it, and she promptly replied that it had never occurred to her. She added that she was extremely sorry and that it had probably in the first instance been the fault of that injudicious dinner.

"Ah, the day of my headache—my miserable headache?" said her visitor. "Yes, very likely that did it. He's so dreadfully good-looking."

"Poor child, he can't help that. Neither can I!" Lady Greyswood ventured to add.

"He comes by it honestly. He seems very nice."

"He's nice enough, but he hasn't a farthing, you know, and his expectations are *nil.*" They considered, they turned the matter about, they wondered what they had better do. In the first place there was no room for doubt; of course Mrs. Knocker hadn't sounded the girl, but a mother, a true mother was never reduced to that. If Fanny was in every relation of life so painfully, so constitutionally awkward, the still depths of her shyness, of her dissimulation even, in such a predicament as this, might easily be imagined. She would give no sign that she could possibly smother, she would say nothing and do nothing, watching herself, poor child, with trepidation; but she would suffer, and some day when the question of her future should really come up—it might after all in the form of some good proposal—they would find themselves beating against a closed door. That was what they had to think of; that was why Mrs. Knocker had come over. Her old friend cross-examined her with a troubled face, but she was very impressive with her reasons, her intuitions.

"I'll send him away in a moment, if you'd like that," Lady Greyswood said at last. "I'll try and get him to go abroad."

Her visitor made no direct reply to this, and no reply at all for some moments. "What does he expect to do—what does he want to do?" she asked.

"Oh, poor boy, he's looking—he's trying to decide. He asks nothing of anyone. If he would only knock at a few doors! But he's too proud."

"Do you call him *very* clever?" Fanny's mother demanded.

"Yes, decidedly—and good and kind and true. But he has been unlucky."

"Of course he can't bear her!" said Mrs. Knocker with a little dry laugh.

Lady Greyswood stared; then she broke out: "Do you mean you'd be willing?———"

"He's very charming."

"Ah, but you must have great ideas."

"He's very well connected," said Mrs. Knocker, snapping the tight elastic on her umbrella.

"Oh, my dear Jane—'connected'!" Lady Greyswood gave a sigh of the sweetest irony.

"He's connected with you, to begin with."

Lady Greyswood put out her hand and held her visitor's for a moment. "Of course it isn't as if he were a different sort of person. Of course I should like it!" she added.

"Does he dislike her *very* much?"

Lady Greyswood looked at her friend with a smile. "He resembles Fanny—he doesn't tell. But what would her father say?" she went on.

"He doesn't know it."

"You've not talked with him?"

Mrs. Knocker hesitated a moment. "He thinks she's all right." Both the ladies laughed a little at the density of men; then the visitor said: "I wanted to see you first."

This circumstance gave Lady Greyswood food for thought; it suggested comprehensively that in spite of a probable deficiency of zeal on the General's part the worthy man would not be the great obstacle. She had begun so quickly to turn over in her mind the various ways in which this new phase of the business might make it possible the real obstacle should be surmounted that she scarcely heard her companion say next: "The General will only want his daughter to be happy. He has no definite ambitions for her. I dare say Maurice could make him like him." It was something more said by her companion about Maurice that sounded sharply through her reverie. "But unless the idea appeals to *him* a bit there's no use talking about it."

At this Lady Greyswood spoke with decision. "It *shall* appeal to him. Leave it to me! Kiss your dear child for me," she added as the ladies embraced and separated.

In the course of the day she made up her mind, and when she again broached the question to her son (it befell that very evening) she felt that she stood on firmer ground. She began by mentioning to him that her dear old friend had the same charming dream—for the girl—that *she* had; she sketched with a light hand a picture of their preconcerted happiness in the union of their children. When he replied that he couldn't for the life of him imagine what the Knockers could see in a poor beggar of a younger son who had publicly come a cropper, she took pains to prove that he was as good as anyone else and much better than many of the young men to whom persons of sense were often willing to confide their daughters. She had been in much tribulation over the circumstance announced to her in the morning, not knowing whether, in her present enterprise, to keep it back or put it forward. If Maurice should happen not to take it in the right way it was the sort of thing that might dish the whole experiment. He might be bored, he might be annoyed, he might be horrified—there was no limit, in such cases, to the perversity, to the possible brutality of even the most amiable man. On the other hand he might be pleased, touched, flattered—if he didn't dislike the girl too much. Lady Greyswood could indeed imagine that it might be unpleasant to know that a person who was disagreeable to you was in love with you; so that there was just that risk to run. She determined to run it only if there should be absolutely no other card to play. Meanwhile she said: "Don't you see, now, how intelligent she is, in her quiet way, and how perfect she is at home—without any nonsense or affectation or ill-nature? She's not a bit stupid, she's remarkably clever. She can do a lot of things; she has no end of talents. Many girls with a quarter of her abilities would make five times the show."

"My dear mother, she's a great swell, I freely admit it. She's far too good for me. What in the world puts it into your two heads that she would look at me?"

At this Lady Greyswood was tempted to speak; but after an instant she said instead: "She *has* looked at you, and you've seen how. You've seen her several times now, and she has been remarkably nice to you."

"Nice? Ah, poor girl, she's frightened to death!"

"Believe me—I read her," Lady Greyswood replied.

"She knows she has money and she thinks I'm after it. She thinks I'm a ravening wolf and she's scared."

"I happen to know as a fact that she's in love with you!" Before she could check herself Lady Greyswood had played her card, and though she held her breath a little after doing so she felt that it had been a good moment. "If I hadn't known it," she hastened further to declare, "I should never have said another word." Maurice burst out laughing—how in the world *did* she know it? When she put the evidence before him she had the pleasure of seeing that he listened without irritation; and this emboldened her to say: "Don't you think you could *try* to like her?"

Maurice was lounging on a sofa opposite to her; jocose but embarrassed, he had thrown back his head, and while he stretched himself his eyes wandered over the upper expanse of the room. "It's very kind of her and of her mother, and I'm much obliged and all that, though a fellow feels rather an ass in talking about such a thing. Of course also I don't pretend—before such a proof of wisdom—that I think her in the least a fool. But, oh, dear——!" And the young man broke off with laughing impatience, as if he had too much to say. His mother waited an instant, then she uttered a persuasive, interrogative sound, and he went on: "It's only a pity she's so awful!"

"So awful?" murmured Lady Greyswood.

"Dear mother, she's about as ugly a woman as ever turned round on you. If there were only just a touch or two less of it!"

Lady Greyswood got up: she stood looking in silence at the tinted shade of the lamp. She remained in this position so long that he glanced at her—he was struck with the sadness in her face. He would have been in error however if he had suspected that this sadness was assumed for the purpose of showing him that she was wounded by his resistance, for the reflection that his last words caused her to make was as disinterested as it was melancholy. Here was an excellent, a charming girl—a girl, she was sure, with a rare capacity for devotion—whose future was reduced to nothing by the mere accident, in her face, of a certain want of drawing. A man could settle her fate with a laugh, could give her away with a snap of his fingers. She seemed to see Maurice administer to poor Fanny's image the little displeased shove with which he would have disposed of an ill-seasoned dish. Moreover he greatly exaggerated. Her heart grew heavy with a sense of the hardness of the lot of women, and when she looked again at her son there were tears in her eyes that startled him. "Poor girl—poor girl!" she simply sighed, in a tone that was to reverberate in his mind and to constitute in doing so a real appeal to his imagination. After a moment she added: "We'll talk no more about her—no, no!"

All the same she went three days later to see Mrs. Knocker and say to her: "My dear creature, I think it's all right."

"Do you mean he'll take us up?"

"He'll come and see you, and you must give him plenty of chances." What Lady Greyswood would have liked to be able to say, crudely and comfortably, was: "He'll try to manage it—he promises to do what he can." What she did say, however, was: "He's greatly prepossessed in the dear child's favour."

"Then I dare say he'll be very nice."

"If I didn't think he'd behave like a gentleman I wouldn't raise a finger. The more he sees of her the more he'll be sure to like her."

"Of course with poor Fanny that's the only thing one can build on," said Mrs. Knocker. "There's so much to get over."

Lady Greyswood hesitated a moment. "Maurice *has* got over it. But I should tell you that at first he doesn't want it known."

"Doesn't want what known?"

"Why, the footing on which he comes. You see it's just the least bit experimental."

"For what do you take me?" asked Mrs. Knocker. "The child shall never dream that anything has passed between us. No more of course shall her father."

"It's too delightful of you to leave it that way," Lady Greyswood replied. "We must surround her happiness with every safeguard."

Mrs. Knocker sat pensive for some moments. "So that if nothing comes of it there's no harm done? That idea—that nothing may come of it—makes one a little nervous," she added.

"Of course I can't absolutely answer for my poor boy!" said Lady Greyswood, with just the faintest ring of impatience. "But he's much affected by what he knows—I told him. That's what moves him."

"He must of course be perfectly free."

"The great thing is for her not to know."

Mrs. Knocker considered. "Are you very sure?" She had apparently had a profounder second thought.

"Why, my dear—with the risk!"

"Isn't the risk, after all, greater the other way? Mayn't it help the matter on, mayn't it do the poor child a certain degree of good, the idea that, as you say, he's prepossessed in her favour? It would perhaps cheer her up, as it were, and encourage her, so that by the very fact of being happier about herself she may make a better impression. That's what she wants, poor thing—to be helped to hold up her head, to take herself more seriously, to believe that people can like her. And fancy, when it's a case of such a beautiful young man who's all ready to!"

"Yes, he's all ready to," Lady Greyswood conceded. "Of course it's a question for your own discretion. I can't advise you, for you know your child. But it seems to me a case for tremendous caution."

"Oh, trust me for that!" said Mrs. Knocker. "We shall be very kind to him," she smiled, as her visitor got up.

"He'll appreciate that. But it's too nice of you to leave it so."

Mrs. Knocker gave a hopeful shrug. "He has only to be civil to Blake!"

"Ah, he isn't a brute!" Lady Greyswood exclaimed, caressing her.

After this she passed a month of no little anxiety. She asked her son no question, and for two or three weeks he offered her no other information than to say two or three times that Miss Knocker really could ride; but she learned from her old friend everything she wanted to know. Immediately after the conference of the two ladies Maurice, in the Row, had taken an opportunity of making up to the girl. She rode every day with her father, and Maurice rode, though possessed of nothing in life to put a leg across; and he had been so well received that this proved the beginning of a custom. He had a canter with the young lady most days in the week, and when they parted it was usually to meet again in the evening. His relations with the household in Ennismore Gardens were indeed not left greatly to his initiative; he became on the spot the subject of perpetual invitations and arrangements, the centre of the friendliest manœuvres; so that Lady Greyswood was struck with Jane Knocker's feverish energy in the good cause—the ingenuity, the bribery, the cunning that an exemplary mother might be inspired to practise. She herself did nothing, she left it all to poor Jane, and this perhaps gave her for the moment a sense of contemplative superiority. She wondered if *she* would in any circumstances have plotted so almost fiercely for one of her children. She was glad her old friend's design had her full approbation; she held her breath a little when she said to herself: "Suppose I hadn't liked it—suppose it had been for Chumleigh!" Chumleigh was the present Lord Greyswood, whom his mother still called by his earlier designation. Fanny Knocker's thirty thousand would have been by no means enough for Chumleigh. Lady Greyswood, in spite of her suspense, was detached enough to be amused when her accomplice told her that "Blake" had said that Maurice really could ride. The two mothers thanked God for the riding—the riding would see them through. Lady

Greyswood had watched Fanny narrowly in the Park, where, in the saddle, she looked no worse than lots of girls. She had no idea how Maurice got his mounts—she knew Chumleigh had none to give him; but there were directions in which she would have encouraged him to incur almost any liability. He was evidently amused and beguiled; he fell into comfortable attitudes on the soft cushions that were laid for him and partook with relish of the dainties that were served; he had his fill of the theatres, of the opera—entertainments of which he was fond. She could see he didn't care for the sort of people he met in Ennismore Gardens, but this didn't matter: so much as that she didn't ask of him. She knew that when he should have something to tell her he would speak; and meanwhile she pretended to be a thousand miles away. The only thing that worried her was that he had dropped photography. She said to Mrs. Knocker more than once: "Does he make love?—that's what I want to know!" to which this lady replied with her incongruous drollery: "My dear, how can I make out? He's so little like Blake!" But she added that she believed Fanny was intensely happy. Lady Greyswood had been struck with the girl's looking so, and she rejoiced to be able to declare in perfectly good faith that she thought her greatly improved. "Didn't I tell you?" returned Mrs. Knocker to this with a certain accent of triumph. It made Lady Greyswood nervous, for she took it to mean that Fanny had had a hint from her mother of Maurice's possible intentions. She was afraid to ask her old friend directly if this were definitely true: poor Fanny's improvement was after all not a gain sufficient to make up for the cruelty that would reside in the sense of being rejected.

One day, in Queen Street, Maurice said in an abrupt, conscientious way: "You were right about Fanny Knocker—she's a remarkably clever and a thoroughly nice girl; a fellow can really talk with her. But oh mother!"

"Well, my dear?"

The young man's face wore a strange smile. "Oh mother!" he expressively, quite tragically repeated. "But it's all right!" he presently added in a different tone, and Lady Greyswood was reassured. This confidence, however, received a shock a little later, on the evening of a day that had been intensely hot. A torrid wave had passed over London, and in the suffocating air the pleasures of the season had put on a purple face. Lady Greyswood, whose own fine lowness of tone no temperature could affect, knew, in her bedimmed drawing-room, exactly the detail of her son's engagements. She pitied him—*she* had managed to keep clear; she had in particular a vision of a distribution of prizes, by one of the princesses, at a big horticultural show; she saw the sweltering starers (and at what, after all?) under a huge glass roof, while there passed before her, in a blur of crimson, the glimpse of uncomfortable cheeks under an erratic white bonnet, together also with the sense that some of Jane Knocker's ideas of pleasure were of the oddest (she had such *lacunes*), and some of the ordeals to which she exposed poor Fanny singularly ill-chosen. Maurice came in, perspiring but pale (nothing could make *him* ugly!) to dress for dinner, and though he was in a great hurry he found time to pant: "Oh mother, what I'm going through for you!"

"Do you mean rushing about so—in this weather? We shall have a change to-night."

"I hope so! There are people for whom it doesn't do at all; ah, not a bit!" said Maurice with a laugh that she didn't fancy. But he went upstairs before she could think of anything to reply, and after he had dressed he passed out without speaking to her again. The next morning, on entering her room, her maid mentioned as a delicate duty that Mr. Glanvil, whose door stood wide open and whose bed was untouched, had apparently not yet come in. While, however, her ladyship was in the first freshness of meditation on this singular fact the morning's letters were brought up, and as it happened that the second envelope she glanced at was addressed in Maurice's hand she was quickly in possession of an explanation still more startling than his absence. He wrote from a club, at nine o'clock the previous evening, to announce that he was taking the night train for the continent. He hadn't dressed for dinner, he had dressed otherwise, and having stuffed a few things with surreptitious haste into a Gladstone bag, had slipped unperceived out of the house and into a hansom. He had sent to Ennismore Gardens, from his club, an apology—a request he should not be waited for; and now he should just have time to get to Charing Cross. He was off he didn't know where, but he was off he did know why. "You'll know why, dear mother too, I think," this wonderful communication continued; "you'll know why, because I haven't deceived you. I've done what I could, but I've broken down. I felt to-day that it was no use; there was a moment, at that beastly exhibition, when I saw it, when the question was settled. The truth rolled over me in a stifling wave. After that I made up my mind there was nothing to do but to bolt. I meant to put it off till to-morrow, and to tell you first, but while I was dressing to-day it struck me irresistibly that my true course is to break now—never to enter the house or go near her again. I was afraid of a scene with you about this. I haven't uttered a word of 'love' to her (heaven save us!) but my position this afternoon became definitely false, and that fact prescribes the course I am taking. You shall hear from me again in a day or two. I have the greatest regard for her, but I can't bear to look at her. I don't care a bit for money, but, hang it, I *must* have beauty! Please send me twenty pounds, *poste restante*, Boulogne."

"What I want, Jane, is to get at this," Lady Greyswood said, later in the day, with an austerity that was sensible even through her tears. "Does the child know, or doesn't she, what was at stake?"

"She hasn't an inkling of it—how should she? I recognised that it was best not to tell her—and I didn't."

On this, as Mrs. Knocker's tears had also flowed, Lady Greyswood kissed her. But she didn't believe her. Fanny herself, however, for the rest of the season, proved inscrutable. "She's a character!" Lady Greyswood reflected with admiration. In September, in Yorkshire, the girl was taken seriously ill.

III

After luncheon at the Crisfords'—the big Sunday banquets of twenty people and a dozen courses—the men, lingering a little in the dining-room, dawdling among displaced chairs and dropped napkins while the ladies rustled away, ended by shuffling in casual pairs up to the studio, where coffee was served and where, presently, before the cigarettes were smoked out, Mrs. Crisford always reappeared to usher in her contingent. The studio was high and handsome, and luncheon at the Crisfords' was, in the common esteem, more amusing than almost anything else in London except dinner. It was Bohemia with excellent service—Bohemia not debtor but creditor. Upstairs the pictures, finished or nearly finished, and arranged in a shining row, gave an obviousness of topic, so that conversation could easily touch bottom. Maurice Glanvil, who had never been in the house before, looked about and wondered; he was struck with the march of civilization—the rise of the social tide. There were new notes in English life, which he caught quickly with his fresh sense; during his long absence—twenty years of France and Italy—all sorts of things had happened. In his youth, in England, artists and authors and actors—people of that general kind—were not nearly so "smart." Maurice Glanvil was forty-nine to-day, and he thought a great deal of his youth. He regretted it, he missed it, he tried to beckon it back; but the differences in London made him feel that it had gone forever. There might perhaps be some sudden compensation in being fifty, some turn of the dim telescope, some view from the brow of the hill; it was a round, gross, stupid number, which probably would make one pompous, make one think one's self venerable. Meanwhile at any rate it was odious to be forty-nine. Maurice observed the young now more than he had ever done; observed them, that is, as the young. He wished he could have had a son, to be twenty with again; his daughter was only eighteen, but fond as he was of her he couldn't live instinctively into her girlishness. It was not that there was not plenty of it, for she was simple, sweet, indefinite, without the gifts that the boy would have had, the gifts—what had become of them now?—that he himself used to have.

The youngest person present, before the ladies came in, was the young man who had sat next to Vera and whom, being on the same side of the long table, he had not had under his eye. Maurice noticed him now, noticed that he was very good-looking, fair and fresh and clean, impeccable in his straight smoothness; also that apparently knowing none of the other guests and moving by himself about the studio with visible interest in the charming things, he had the modesty of his age and of his position. He had however something more besides, which had begun to prompt this observer to speak to him in order to hear the sound of his voice—a strange, elusive resemblance, lost in the profile but flickering straight out of the full face, to someone Maurice had known. For a minute Glanvil was worried by it—he had a sense that a name would suddenly come to him if he should see the lips in motion; but as he was on the point of laying the ghost by an experiment Mrs. Crisford led in her companions. His daughter was among them, and in company, as he was constantly anxious about her appearance and her attitude, she had at moments the faculty of drawing his attention from everything else. The poor child, the only fruit of his odd, romantic union, the *coup de foudre* of his youth, with her strangely beautiful mother, whose own mother had been a Russian and who had died in giving birth to her—his short, colourless, insignificant Vera was excessively, incorrigibly plain. She had been the disappointment of his life, but he greatly pitied her. Her want of beauty, with her antecedents, had been one of the strangest tricks of fate; she was acutely conscious of it and, being good and docile, would have liked to please. She did sometimes, to her father's delight, in spite of everything; she had been educated abroad, on foreign lines, near her mother's people. He had brought her to England to take her out, to do what he could for her; but he was not unaware that in England her manners, which had been thought very pretty on the continent, would strike some persons as artificial. They were exactly what her mother's had been; they made up to a certain extent for the want of other resemblance. An extreme solicitude at any rate as to the impression they might make was the source of his habit, in London, of watching her covertly. He tried to see at a given moment how she looked, if she were happy; it was always with an intention of encouragement, and there was a frequent exchange between them of little invisible affectionate signs. She wore charming clothes, but she was terribly short; in England the girls were gigantic and it was only the tallest who were noticed. Their manners, alas, had nothing to do with it—many of them indeed hadn't any manners. As soon as he had got near Vera he said to her, scanning her through his single glass from head to foot:

"Who is the young man who sat next you? the one at the other end of the room."

"I don't know his name, papa—I didn't catch it."

"Was he civil—did he talk to you?"

"Oh, a great deal, papa—about all sorts of things."

Something in the tone of her voice made him look with greater intensity and even with greater tenderness than usual into her little dim green eyes. "Then you're all right—you're getting on?"

She gave her effusive smile—the one that perhaps wouldn't do in England. "Oh beautifully, papa—everyone's so kind."

She never complained, was a brave little optimist, full of sweet resources; but he had detected to-day as soon as he looked at her the particular shade of her content. It made him continue, after an hesitation: "He didn't say anything about his relations—anything that could give you a clue?"

Vera thought a moment. "Not that I can remember—unless that Mr. Crisford is painting the portrait of his mother. Ah, there it is!" the girl exclaimed, looking across the room at a large picture on an easel, which the young man had just approached and from which their host had removed the drapery that covered it. Maurice Glanvil had observed this drapery, and as the artist unveiled the canvas with a flourish he saw that he had been waiting for the ladies to show it, to produce a surprise, a grand effect. Everyone moved toward it, and Maurice, with his daughter beside him, recognised that the production, a portrait, was striking, a great success for Crisford—the figure, down to the knees, with an extraordinary look of life, of a tall, handsome woman of middle age, in full dress, in black. Yet he saw it for the moment vaguely, through a preoccupation, that of a discovery which he had just made and which had recalled to him an incident of his youth—his juxtaposition, in London, at a dinner, to a girl, insurmountably charmless to him, who had fallen in love with him (so that she was nearly to die of it), within the first five minutes, before he had even spoken; as he had subsequently learned from a communication made him by his poor mother—a reminder uttered with a pointless bitterness that he had failed to understand and accompanied with unsuspected details, much later—too late, long after his marriage and shortly before her death. He said to himself that he must look out, and he wondered if poor Vera would also be insurmountably charmless to the good-looking young man. "But what a likeness, papa—what a likeness!" he heard her murmur at his elbow with suppressed excitement.

"How can you tell, my dear, if you haven't seen her?"

"I mean to the gentleman—the son."

Everyone was exclaiming "How wonderfully clever—how beautiful!" and under cover of the agitation and applause Maurice Glanvil had drawn nearer the picture. The movement had brought him close to the young man of whom he had been talking with Vera and who, with his happy eyes on the painted figure, seemed to smile in acknowledgment of the artist's talent and of the sitter's charm.

"Do you know who the lady is?" Maurice said to him.

He turned his bright face to his interlocutor. "She's my mother—Mrs. Tregent. Isn't it wonderful?"

His eyes, his lips, his voice flashed a light into Glanvil's uncertainty—the tormenting resemblance was simply a prolonged echo of Fanny Knocker, in whose later name, precisely, he recognised the name pronounced by the young man. Maurice Glanvil stared in some bewilderment; this stately, splendid lady, with a face so vivid that it was handsome, was what that unfortunate girl had become? The eyes, as if they picked him out, looked at him strangely from the canvas; the face, with all its difference, asserted itself, and he felt himself turning as red as if he had been in the presence of the original. Young Tregent, pleased and proud, had given way to the pressing spectators, placing himself at Vera's other side; and Maurice heard the girl exclaim to him in one of her pretty effusions: "How beautiful she must be, and how amiable!"

"She is indeed—it's not a bit flattered." And while Maurice still stared, more and more mystified—for "flattered, flattered!" was the unspoken solution in which he had instantly taken refuge—his neighbour continued: "I wish you could know her—you must; she's delightful. She couldn't come here to-day—they asked her: she has people lunching at home."

"I should be so glad; perhaps we may meet her somewhere," said Vera.

"If I ask her and if you'll let her I'm sure she'll come to see you," the young man responded. Maurice had glanced at him while the face of the portrait watched them with the oddest, the grimmest effect. He was filled with a confusion of feelings, asking himself half-a-dozen questions at once. Was young Tregent, with his attentive manner, "making up" to Vera? was he going out of his way in answering for his mother's civility? Little did he know what he was taking on himself! Above all was Fanny Knocker to-day this extraordinary figure—extraordinary in the light of the early plainness that had made him bolt? He became conscious of an extreme curiosity, an irresistible desire to see her.

"Oh, papa," said Vera, "Mr. Tregent's so kind; he's so good as to promise us a visit from his mother."

The young man's friendly eyes were still on the child's face. "I'll tell her all about you. Oh, if I ask her she'll come!" he repeated.

"Does she do everything you ask her?" the girl inquired.

"She likes to know my friends!"

Maurice hesitated, wondering if he were in the presence of a smooth young humbug to whom compliments cost nothing, or in that of an impression really made—made by his little fluttered, unpopular Vera. He had a horror of exposing his child to risks, but his curiosity was greater than his caution. "Your mother mustn't come to us—it's our duty to go to her," he said to Mr. Tregent; "I had the honour of knowing her—a long time ago. Her mother and mine were intimate friends. Be so good as to mention my name to her, that of Maurice Glanvil, and to tell her how glad I have been to make your acquaintance. And now, my dear child," he added to Vera, "we must take leave."

During the rest of that day it never occurred to him that there might be an awkwardness in his presenting himself, even after many years, before a person with whom he had broken as he had broken with Fanny Knocker. This was partly because he held, justly enough, that he had never committed himself, and partly because the intensity of his desire to measure with his own eyes the change represented—misrepresented perhaps—by the picture was a force greater than any embarrassment. His mother had told him that the poor girl had cruelly suffered, but there was no present intensity in that idea. With her expensive portrait, her grand air, her handsome son, she somehow embodied success, whereas he himself, standing for mere bereavement and disappointment, was a failure not to be surpassed. With Vera that evening he was very silent; she saw him smoke endless cigarettes and wondered what he was thinking of. She guessed indeed, but she was too subtle a little person to attempt to fall in with his thoughts or to be willing to betray her own by asking him random questions about Mrs. Tregent. She had expressed as they came away from their luncheon-party a natural surprise at the coincidence of his having known the mother of her amusing neighbour, but the only other words that dropped from her on the subject were contained in a question that, before she went to bed, she put to him with abrupt gaiety, while she carefully placed a marker in a book she had not been reading.

"When is it then that we're to call upon this wonderful old friend?"

He looked at her through the smoke of his cigarette. "I don't know. We must wait a little, to allow her time to give some sign."

"Oh, I see!" And Vera took leave of him with one of her sincere little kisses.

IV

He had not long to wait for the sign from Mrs. Tregent; it arrived the very next morning in the shape of an invitation to dinner. This invitation was immediately accepted, but a fortnight was still to intervene—a trial to Maurice Glanvil's patience. The promptitude of the demonstration gave him pleasure—it showed him no bitterness had survived. What place was there indeed for resentment, since she had married and given birth to children and thought so well of the face God had conferred on her as to wish to hand it on to her posterity? Her husband was in Parliament, or had been—that came back to him from his mother's story. He caught himself reverting to her with a frequency that surprised him; he was haunted by the image of that bright, strong woman on Crisford's canvas, in whom there was just enough of Fanny Knocker to put a sort of defiance into the difference. He wanted to see it again, and his opportunity was at hand in the form of a visit to Mrs. Crisford. He called on this lady, without his daughter, four days after he had lunched with her, and, finding her at home, he presently led the conversation to the portrait and to his ardent desire for another glimpse of it. Mrs. Crisford gratified this eagerness—perhaps he struck her as a possible sitter; it was late in the afternoon and her husband was out: she led him into the studio. Mrs. Tregent, splendid and serene, stood there as if she had been watching for him. There was no doubt the picture was a masterpiece. Maurice had mentioned that he had known the original years before and then had lost sight of her. He questioned his hostess with artful detachment.

"What sort of a person has she become—agreeable, popular?"

"Everyone adores her—she's so clever."

"Really—remarkably?"

"Extraordinarily—one of the cleverest women I've ever known, and quite one of the most charming."

Maurice looked at the portrait—at the super-subtle smile which seemed to tell him Mrs. Tregent knew they were talking about her; a kind of smile he had never expected to live to see in Fanny Knocker's eyes. Then he asked: "Has she literally become as handsome as that?"

Mrs. Crisford hesitated. "She's beautiful."

"Beautiful?" Maurice echoed.

"What shall I say? It's a peculiar charm! It's her spirit. One sees that her life has been beautiful in spite of her sorrows!" Mrs. Crisford added.

"What sorrows has she had?" Maurice coloured a little as soon as he had spoken.

"Oh, lots of deaths. She has lost her husband; she has lost several children."

"Ah, that's new to me. Was her marriage happy?"

"It must have been for Mr. Tregent. If it wasn't for her, no one ever knew."

"But she has a son," said Maurice.

"Yes, the only one—such a dear. She thinks all the world of him."

At this moment a message was brought to Mrs. Crisford, and she asked to be excused while she went to say a word to someone who was waiting. Maurice Glanvil in this way was left alone for five minutes with the intensity of the presence evoked by the artist. He found himself agitated, excited by it: the face of the portrait was so intelligent and conscious that as he stood there he felt as if some strange communication had taken place between his being and Mrs. Tregent's. The idea made him nervous: he moved about the room and ended by turning his back. Mrs. Crisford reappeared, but he soon took leave of her; and when he had got home (he had settled himself in South Kensington, in a little undiscriminated house which he had hated from the first), he learned from his daughter that she had had a visit from young Tregent. He had asked first for Mr. Glanvil and then, in the second instance, for herself, telling her when admitted, as if to attenuate his possible indiscretion, that his mother had charged him to try to see her even if he should not find her father. Vera had never before received a gentleman alone, and the incident had left traces of emotion. "Poor little thing!" Maurice said to himself: he always took a melancholy view of any happiness of his daughter's, tending to believe, in his pessimism, that it could only lead to some refinement of humiliation. He encouraged her however to talk about young Tregent, who, according to her account, had been extravagantly amusing. He had said moreover that his mother was tremendously impatient to renew such an old acquaintance. "Why in the world doesn't she, then?" Maurice asked himself; "why doesn't she come and see Vera?" He reflected afterwards that such an expectation was unreasonable, but it represented at the moment a kind of rebellion of his conscience. Then, as he had begun to be a little ashamed of his curiosity, he liked to think that Mrs. Tregent would have quite as much. On the morrow he knocked at her door—she lived in a "commodious" house in Manchester Square—and had the satisfaction, as he had chosen his time carefully, of learning that she had just come in.

Upstairs, in a high, quiet, old-fashioned drawing-room, she was before him. What he saw was a tall woman in black, in her bonnet, with a white face, smiling intensely—smiling and smiling before she spoke. He quickly perceived that she was agitated and was making an heroic effort, which would presently be successful, not to show it. But it was above all clear to him that she wasn't Fanny Knocker—was simply another person altogether. She had nothing in common with Fanny Knocker—it was impossible to meet her on the ground of any former acquaintance. What acquaintance had he ever had with this graceful, harmonious, expressive English matron, whose smile had a singular radiance? That rascal of a Crisford had done her such perfect justice that he felt as if he had before him the portrait of which the image in the studio had been the original. There were nevertheless things to be said, and they said them on either side, sinking together, with friendly exclamations and exaggerated laughs, on the sofa, where her nearness seemed the span of all the distance that separated her from the past. The phrase that hummed through everything, to his sense, was his own inarticulate "How could I have known? how could I have known?" How could he have foreseen that time and life and happiness (it was probably more than anything happiness), would transpose her into such a different key? Her whole personality revealed itself from moment to moment as something so agreeable that even after all these years he felt himself blushing for the crass stupidity of his mistake. Yes, he was turning red, and she could see it and would know why: a perception that could only constitute for her a magnificent triumph, a revenge. All his natural and acquired coolness, his experience of life, his habit of society, everything that contributed to make him a man of the world, were of no avail to cover his confusion. He took refuge from it almost angrily in trying to prove to himself that she had on a second look a likeness to the ugly girl he had not thought good enough—in trying to trace Fanny Knocker in her fair, ripe bloom, the fine irregularity of her features. To put his finger on the identity would make him feel better. Some of the facts of the girl's crooked face were still there—conventional beauty was absent; but the proportions and relations had changed, and the expression and the spirit: she had accepted herself or ceased to care—had found oblivion and activity and appreciation. What Maurice mainly discovered however in this intenser observation was an attitude of hospitality toward himself which immediately effaced the presumption of "triumph." Vulgar vanity was far from her, and the grossness of watching her effect upon him: she was watching only the lost vision that had come back, the joy that, if for a single hour, she had found again. She herself had no measure of the alteration that struck him, and there was no substitution for her in the face that her deep eyes seemed to brush with their hovering. Presently they were talking like old friends, and before long each was in possession of the principal facts concerning the other. Many things had come and gone and the common fate had pressed them hard. Her parents were dead, and her husband and her first-born children. He, on his side, had lost his mother and his wife. They matched bereavements and compared bruises, and in the way she expressed herself there was a charm which forced him, as he wondered, to remember that Fanny Knocker had at least been intelligent.

"I wish I could have seen your wife—you must tell me all about her," she said. "Haven't you some portraits?"

"Some poor little photographs. I'll show them to you. She was very pretty and very gentle; she was also very un-English. But she only lived a year. She wasn't clever and accomplished—like you."

"Ah, me; you don't know *me!*"

"No, but I want to—oh particularly. I'm prepared to give a good deal of time to the study."

"We must be friends," said Mrs. Tregent. "I shall take an extraordinary interest in your daughter."

"She'll be grateful for it. She's a good little reasonable thing, without a scrap of beauty."

"You care greatly for that," said Mrs. Tregent.

He hesitated a moment. "Don't you?"

She smiled at him with her basking candour. "I used to. That's my husband," she added, with an odd, though evidently accidental, inconsequence. She had reached out to a table for a photograph in a silver frame. "He was very good to me."

Maurice saw that Mr. Tregent had been many years older than his wife—a prosperous, prosaic, parliamentary person whom she couldn't impose on a man of the world. He sat an hour, and they talked of the mutilated season of their youth: he wondered at the things she remembered. In this little hour he felt his situation change—something strange and important take place: he seemed to see why he had come back to England. But there was an implication that worried him—it was in the very air, a reverberation of that old assurance of his mother's. He wished to clear the question up—it would matter for the beginning of a new friendship. Had she had any sense of injury when he took to his heels, any glimpse of the understanding on which he had begun to come to Ennismore Gardens? He couldn't find out to-day except by asking her, which, at their time of life, after so many years and consolations, would be legitimate and even amusing. When he took leave of her he held her hand a moment, hesitating; then he brought out:

"Did they ever tell you—a hundred years ago—that between your mother and mine there was a great question of our marrying?"

She stared—she broke into a laugh. "*Was* there?"

"Did you ever know it? Did you ever suspect it?"

She hesitated and, for the first time since he had been in the room, ceased for an instant to look straight at him. She only answered, still laughing however: "Poor dears—they were altogether too deep!"

She evidently wished to convey that she had never known. Maurice was a little disappointed: at present he would have preferred her knowledge. But as he walked home across the park, through Kensington Gardens, he felt it impossible to believe in her ignorance.

V

At the end of a month he broke out to her. "I can't get over it, it's so extraordinary—the difference between your youth and your maturity!"

"Did you expect me to be an eternal child?" Mrs. Tregent asked composedly.

"No, it isn't that." He stopped—it would be difficult to explain.

"What is it then?" she inquired, with her systematic refusal to acknowledge a complication. There was always, to Maurice Glanvil's ear, in her impenetrability to allusion, the faintest, softest glee, and it gave her on this occasion the appearance of recognising his difficulty and being amused at it. She would be excusable to be a little cold-blooded. He really knew however that the penalty was all in his own reflections, for it had not taken him even a month to perceive that she was supremely, almost strangely indulgent. There was nothing he was ready to say that she might not hear, and her absence of coquetry was a remarkable rest to him.

"It isn't what I expected—it's what I didn't expect. To say exactly what I mean, it's the way you've improved."

"I've improved? I'm so glad!"

"Surely you've been aware of it—you've been conscious of the transformation."

"As an improvement? I don't know. I've been conscious of changes enough—of all the stages and strains and lessons of life. I've been aware of growing old, and I hold, in dissent from the usual belief, that there's no fool like a young fool. One is never, I suppose, such a fool as one *has* been, and that may count perhaps as amelioration. But I can't flatter myself that I've had two different identities. I've had to make one, such as it is, do for everything. I think I've been happier than I originally supposed I should be—and yet I had my happiness too as a girl. At all events if you were to scratch me, as they say, you'd still find——" She paused a moment, and he really hung upon her lips: there was such a charm of tone in whatever she said. "You'd still find, underneath, the blowsy girl——" With this she again checked herself and, slightly to his surprise, gave a nervous laugh.

"The blowsy girl?" he repeated, with an artlessness of interrogation that made her laugh again.

"Whom you went with that hot day to see the princess give the prizes."

"Oh yes—that dreadful day!" he answered gravely, musingly, with the whole scene pictured by her words and without contesting the manner in which she qualified herself. It was the nearest allusion that had passed between them to that crudest conception of his boyhood, his flight from Ennismore Gardens. Almost every day for a month he had come to see her, and they had talked of a thousand things; never yet however had they made any explicit mention of this remote instance of premature wisdom. Moreover if he now felt the need of going back it was not to be apologetic, to do penance; he had nothing to explain, for his behaviour, as he considered it, still struck him, given the circumstances, as natural. It was to himself indeed that explanations were owing, for he had been the one who had been most deceived. He liked Mrs. Tregent better than he had ever liked a woman—that is he liked her for more reasons. He had liked his poor little wife only for one, which was after all no reason at all: he had been in love with her. In spite of the charm that the renewal of acquaintance with his old friend had so unexpectedly added to his life there was a vague torment in his relation with her, the sense of a revenge (oh a very kind one!) to take, a haunting idea that he couldn't pacify. He could still feel sore at the trick that had been played him. Even after a month the curiosity with which he had approached her was not assuaged; in a manner indeed it had only borrowed force from all she had insisted on doing for him. She was literally doing everything now; gently, gaily, with a touch so familiar that protestations on his part would have been pedantic, she had taken his life in hand. Rich as she was she had known how to give him lessons in economy; she had taught him how to manage in London on his means. A month ago his servants had been horrid—to-day they were the best he had ever known. For Vera she was plainly a providence—her behaviour to Vera was transcendent.

He had privately made up his mind that Vera had in truth had her *coup de foudre*—that if she had had a chance she would have laid down her little life for Arthur Tregent; yet two circumstances, he could perceive, had helped to postpone, to attenuate even somewhat, her full consciousness of what had befallen her. One of these influences had been the prompt departure of the young man from London; the other was simply the diversion produced by Mrs. Tregent's encompassing art. It had had immediate consequences for the child: it was like a drama in perpetual climaxes. This surprising benefactress rejoiced in her society, took her "out," treated her as if there were mysterious injustices to repair. Vera was agitated not a little by such a change in her life; she had English kindred enough, uncles and aunts and cousins; but she had felt herself lost in her father's family and was principally aware, among them, of their strangeness and their indifference. They affected her mainly as mere number and stature. Mrs. Tregent's was a performance unpromised and uninterrupted, and the girl desired to know if all English people took so generous a view of friendship. Maurice laughed at this question and, without meeting his daughter's eyes, answered in the negative. Vera guessed so many things that he didn't know what she would be guessing next. He saw her caught up to the blue like Ganymede, and surrendered her contentedly. She had been the occupation of his life, yet to Mrs. Tregent he was willing to part with her; this lady was the only person of whom he would not have been jealous. Even in the young man's absence moreover Vera lived with the son of the house and breathed his air; Manchester Square was full of him, his photograph was on every table. How often she spoke of him to his mother Maurice had no means of knowing, nor whether Mrs. Tregent encouraged such a topic; he had reason to believe indeed that there were reserves on either side, and he felt that he could trust his old friend's prudence as much as her liberality. The attitude of forbearance from rash allusions, which was Maurice's own, could not at any rate keep Arthur from being a presence in the little drama which had begun for them all, as the older man was more and more to recognise with nervous prefigurements, on that occasion at the Crisfords'.

Arthur Tregent had gone to Ireland to spend a few weeks with an old university friend—the gentleman indeed, at Cambridge, had been his tutor—who had lately, in a district classified as "disturbed," come into a bewildering heritage. He had chosen in short for a study of the agrarian question on the spot the moment of the year when London was most absorbing. Maurice Glanvil made no remark to his mother on this anomaly, and she offered him no explanation of it; they talked in fact of almost everything except Arthur. Mrs. Tregent had to her constant visitor the air of feeling that she owed him in relation to her son an apology which she had not the materials for making. It was certainly a high standard of courtesy that would suggest to her that he ought to have put himself out for these social specimens; but it was obvious that her standard was high. Maurice Glanvil smiled when he thought to what bare civility the young man would have deemed himself held had he known of a certain passage of private history. But he knew nothing—Maurice was sure of that; his reason for going away had been quite another matter. That Vera's brooding parent should have had such an insight into the young man's motives is a proof of the amount of reflection that he devoted to him. He had not seen much of him and in truth he found him provoking, but he was haunted by the odd analogy of which he had had a glimpse on their first encounter. The late Mr. Tregent had had "interests in the north," and the care of them had naturally devolved upon his son, who by the mother's account had shown an admirable capacity for business. The late Mr. Tregent had also been actively political, and it was fondly hoped, in Manchester Square at least, that the day was not distant when his heir would, in turn and as a representative of the same respectabilities, speak reported words in debate.

Maurice himself, vague about the House of Commons, had nothing to say against his making a figure there. Accordingly if these natural gifts continued to remind him of his own fastidiously clever youth, it was with the difference that Arthur Tregent's cleverness struck him as much the greater of the two. If the changes in England were marked this indeed was in general one of them, that the sharp young men were still sharper than of yore. When they had ability at any rate they showed it all; Maurice would never have pretended that he had shown all his. He had not cared whether anyone knew it. It was not however this superior intensity which provoked him, and poor young Tregent could not be held responsible for his irritation. If the circumstance in which they most resembled each other was the disposition to escape from plain girls who aspired to them, such a characteristic, as embodied in the object of Vera's admiration, was purely interesting, was even amusing, to Vera's father; but it would have gratified him to be able to ascertain from Mrs. Tregent whether, to her knowledge, her son thought his child really repulsive, and what annoyed him was the fact that such an inquiry was practically impossible. Arthur was provoking in short because he had an advantage—an advantage residing in the fact that his mother's friend couldn't ask questions about him without appearing to indulge in hints and overtures. The idea of this officiousness was odious to Maurice Glanvil; so that he confined himself to meditating in silence on the happiness it would be for poor Vera to marry a beautiful young man with a fortune and a future.

Though the opportunity for this recreation—it engaged much of his time—should be counted as one of the pleasant results of his intimacy with Mrs. Tregent, yet the sense, perverse enough, that he had a ground of complaint against her subsisted even to the point of finally steadying him while he expressed his grievance. This happened in the course of one of those afternoon hours that had now become indispensable to him—hours of belated tea and egotistical talk in the long summer light and the chastened roar of London.

"No, it wasn't fair," he said, "and I wasn't well used—a hundred years ago. I'm sore about it now; you ought to have notified me, to have instructed me. Why didn't you, in common honesty? Why didn't my poor mother, who was so eager and shrewd? Why didn't yours? She used to talk to me. Heaven forgive me for saying it, but our mothers weren't up to the mark! You may tell me they didn't know; to which I reply that mine was universally supposed, and by me in particular, to know everything that could be known. No, it wasn't well managed, and the consequence has been this odious discovery, an awful shock to a man of my time of life and under the effect of which I now speak to you, that for a quarter of a century I've been a fool."

"What would you have wished us to do?" Mrs. Tregent asked as she gave him another cup of tea.

"Why, to have said 'Wait, wait—at any price; have patience and hold on!' They ought to have told me, *you* ought to have told me, that your conditions at that time were a temporary phase and that you would infallibly break your shell. You ought to have warned me, they ought to have warned me, that there would be wizardry in the case, that you were to be the subject, at a given moment, of a transformation absolutely miraculous. I couldn't know it by inspiration; I measured you by the common law—how could I do anything else? But it wasn't kind to leave me in error."

Maurice Glanvil treated himself without scruple to this fine ironic flight, this sophistry which eased his nerves, because though it brought him nearer than he had yet come to putting his finger, visibly to Mrs. Tregent, on the fact that he had once tried to believe he could marry her and had found her too ugly, their present relation was so extraordinary and his present appreciation so liberal as to make almost any freedom excusable, especially as his companion had the advantage of being to all intents and purposes a different person from the one he talked of, while he suffered the ignominy of being the same.

"There has been no miracle," said Mrs. Tregent after a moment. "I've never known anything but the common, ah the very common, law, and anything that I may have become only the common things have made me."

He shook his head. "You wore a disfiguring mask, a veil, a disguise. One fine day you dropped them all and showed the world the real creature."

"It wasn't one fine day—it was little by little."

"Well, one fine day I saw the result; the process doesn't matter. To arrive at a goal invisible from the starting-point is no doubt an incident in the life of a certain number of women. But what is absolutely unprecedented is to have traversed such a distance."

"Hadn't I a single redeeming point?" Mrs. Tregent demanded.

He hesitated a little, and while he hesitated she looked at him. Her look was but of an instant, but it told him everything, told him, in one misty moonbeam, all she had known of old. She had known perfectly—she had been as conscious of the conditions of his experiment as of the invincibility of his repugnance. Whether her mother had betrayed him didn't matter; she had read everything clear and had had to accept the cruel truth. He was touched as he had never been by that moment's communication; he was, unexpectedly, almost awestruck, for there was something still more in it than he had guessed. "I was letting my fancy play just now," he answered, apologetically. "It was I who was wanting—it was I who was the idiot!"

"Don't say that. You were so kind." And hereupon Mrs. Tregent startled her visitor by bursting into tears.

She recovered herself indeed, and they forbore on that occasion, in the interest of the decorum expected of persons of their age and in their circumstances, to rake over these smouldering ashes; but such a conversation had made a difference, and from that day onward Maurice Glanvil was awake to the fact that he had been the passion of this extraordinary woman's life. He felt humiliated for an hour, but after that his pleasure was almost as great as his wonder. For wonder there was plenty of room, but little by little he saw how things had come to pass. She was not subjected to the ordeal of telling him or to the abasement of any confession, but day by day he sounded, with a purity of gratitude that renewed, in his spirit, the sources of youth, the depths of everything that her behaviour implied. Of such a studied tenderness as she showed him the roots could only be in some unspeakably sacred past. She had not to explain, she had not to clear up inconsistencies, she had only to let him be with her. She had striven, she had accepted, she had conformed, but she had thought of him every day of her life. She had taken up duties and performed them, she had banished every weakness and practised every virtue, but the still, hidden flame had never been quenched. His image had interposed, his reality had remained, and she had never denied herself the sweetness of hoping that she should see him again and that she should know him. She had never raised a little finger for it, but fortune had answered her prayer. Women were capable of these mysteries of sentiment, these intensities of fidelity and there were moments in which Maurice Glanvil's heart beat strangely before a vision really so sublime. He seemed to understand now by what miracle Fanny Knocker had been beautified—the miracle of heroic docilities and accepted pangs and vanquished egotisms. It had never come in a night, but it had come by living for others. She was living for others still; it was impossible for him to see anything else at last than that she was living for him. The time of passion was over, but the time of service was long. When all this became vivid to him he felt that he couldn't recognise it enough and yet that recognition might only be tacit and, as it were, circuitous. He couldn't say to her even humorously "It's very kind of you to be in love with such a donkey," for these words would have implied somehow that he had rights—an attitude from which his renovated delicacy shrank. He bowed his head before such charity and seemed to see moreover that Mrs. Tregent's desire to befriend him was a feeling independent of any prospect of gain and indifferent to any chance of reward. It would be described vulgarly, after so much had come and gone, as the state of being "in love"—the state of the instinctive and the simple, which they both had left far behind; so that there was a certain sort of reciprocity which would almost constitute an insult to it.

VI

He soared on these high thoughts till, toward the end of July (Mrs. Tregent stayed late in town—she was awaiting her son's return) he made the discovery that to some persons, perhaps indeed to many, he had all the air of being in love. This image was flashed back to him from the irreverent lips of a lady who knew and admired Mrs. Tregent and who professed amusement at his surprise, at his artless declaration that he had no idea he had made himself conspicuous. She assured him that everyone was talking about him—though people after all had a tenderness for elderly romance; and she left him divided between the acute sense that he was comical (he had a horror of that) and the pale perception of something that he could "help" still less. At the end of a few hours of reflection he had sacrificed the penalty to the privilege; he was about to be fifty, and he knew Fanny Knocker's age—no one better; but he cared no straw for vulgar judgments and moreover could think of plenty of examples of unions admired even after longer delays. For three days he enjoyed the luxury of admitting to himself without reserve how indispensable she had become to him; as the third drew to a close he was more nervous than really he had ever been in his life, for this was the evening on which, after many hindrances, Mrs. Tregent had agreed to dine with him. He had planned the occasion for a month—he wanted to show her how well he had learned from her how to live on his income. Her occupations had always interposed—she was teaching him new lessons; but at last she gave him the joy of sitting at his table. At the evening's end he begged her to remain after the others, and he asked one of the ladies who had been present, and who was going to a pair of parties, to be so good as to take Vera away. This indeed had been arranged in advance, and when, in the discomposed drawing-room, of which the windows stood open to the summer night, he was alone with his old friend, he saw in her face that she knew it had been arranged. He saw more than this—that she knew what he was waiting to say and that if, after a visible reluctance, she had consented to come, it was in order to meet him, with whatever effort, on the ground he had chosen—meet him once and then leave it forever. This was why, without interrupting him, but before he had finished, putting out her hand to his own, with a strange clasp of refusal, she was ready to show him, in a woeful but beautiful headshake to which nothing could add, that it was impossible at this time of day for them to marry. She stayed only a moment, but in that moment he had to accept the knowledge that by as much as it might have been of old, by so much might it never be again. After she had gone he walked up and down the drawing-room half the night. He sent the servants to bed, he blew out the candles; the forsaken place was lighted only by the lamps in the street. He gave himself the motive of waiting for Vera to come back, but in reality he threshed about in the darkness because his cheeks had begun to burn. There was a sting for him in Mrs. Tregent's refusal, and this sting was sharper even than the disappointment of his desire. It was a reproach to his delicacy; it made him feel as if he had been an ass for the second time. When she was young and free his faith had been too poor and his perceptions too dense; he had waited to show her that he only bargained for certainties and only recognised success. He dropped into a chair at last and sat there a long time, his elbows on his knees, his face in his hands, trying to cover up his humiliation, waiting for it to ebb. As the sounds of the night died away it began to come back to him that she had given him a promise to which a rich meaning could be attached. What was it that before going away she had said about Vera, in words he had been at the moment too disconcerted to take in? Little by little he reconstructed these words with comfort; finally, when after hearing a carriage stop at the door he hastily pulled himself together and went down to admit his daughter, the sight of the child on his threshold, as the brougham that had restored her drove away, brought them all back in their generosity.

"Have you danced?" he asked.

She hesitated. "A little, papa."

He knew what that meant—she had danced once. He followed her upstairs in silence; she had not wasted her time—she had had her humiliation. Ah, clearly she was too short! Yet on the landing above, where her bedroom candle stood, she tried to be gay with him, asking him about his own party and whether the people had stayed late.

"Mrs. Tregent stayed after the others. She spoke very kindly of you."

The girl looked at her father with an anxiety that showed through her smile. "What did she say?"

He hesitated, as Vera had done a moment before. "That you must be our compensation."

His daughter's eyes, still wondering, turned away. "What did she mean?"

"That it's all right, darling!" And he supplied the deficiencies of this explanation with a long kiss for good-night.

The next day he went to see Mrs. Tregent, who wore the air of being glad to have something at once positive and pleasant to say. She announced immediately that Arthur was coming back.

"I congratulate you." Then, as they exchanged one of their looks of unreserved recognition, Maurice added: "Now it's for Vera and me to go."

"To go?"

"Without more delay. It's high time we should take ourselves off."

Mrs. Tregent was silent a moment. "Where shall you go?"

"To our old haunts, abroad. We must see some of our old friends. We shall spend six months away."

"Then what becomes of *my* months?"

"Your months?"

"Those it's all arranged she's to spend at Blankley." Blankley was Mrs. Tregent's house in Derbyshire, and she laughed as she went on: "Those that I spoke of last evening. Don't look as if we had never discussed it and settled it!"

"What shall I do without her?" Maurice Glanvil presently demanded.

"What will you do *with* her?" his hostess replied, with a world of triumphant meaning. He was not prepared to say, in the sense of her question, and he took refuge in remarking that he noted her avoidance of any suggestion that he too would be welcome in Derbyshire; which led her to continue, with unshrinking frankness: "Certainly, I don't want you a bit. Leave us alone."

"Is it safe?"

"Of course I can't absolutely answer for anything, but at least it will be safer than with *you*," said Mrs. Tregent.

Maurice Glanvil turned this over. "Does he dislike me?"

"What an idea!"

But the question had brought the colour to her face, and the sight of this, with her evasive answer, kindled in Maurice's heart a sudden relief, a delight almost, that was strange enough. Arthur was in opposition, plainly, and that was why he had so promptly quitted London, that was why Mrs. Tregent had refused Mr. Glanvil. The idea was an instant balm. "He'd be quite right, poor fellow!" Maurice declared. "I'll go abroad alone."

"Let me keep her six months," said Mrs. Tregent. "I'll try it—I'll try it!"

"I wouldn't interfere for the world."

"It's an immense responsibility; but I should like so to succeed."

"She's an angel!" Maurice said.

"That's what gives me courage."

"But she mustn't dream of any plot," he added.

"For what do you take me?" Mrs. Tregent exclaimed with a smile which lightened up for him intensely that far-away troubled past as to which she had originally baffled his inquiry.

The joy of perceiving in an aversion to himself a possible motive for Arthur's absence was so great in him that before he took leave of her he ventured to say to his old friend: "Does he like her at all?"

"He likes her very much."

Maurice remembered how much he had liked Fanny Knocker and been willing to admit it to his mother; but he presently observed: "Of course he can't think her in the least pretty."

"As you say, she's an angel," Mrs. Tregent rejoined.

"She would pass for one better if she were a few inches taller."

"It doesn't matter," said Mrs. Tregent.

"One must remember that in that respect, at her age, she won't change," Maurice pursued, wondering after he had spoken whether he had pressed upon the second pronoun.

"No, she won't change. But she's a darling!" Mrs. Tregent exclaimed; and it was in these meagre words, which were only half however of what passed between them, that an extraordinary offer was made and accepted. They were so ready to understand each other that no insistence and no professions now were necessary, and that Maurice Glanvil had not even broken into a murmur of gratitude at this quick revelation of his old friend's beautiful conception of a nobler remedy—the endeavour to place their union outside themselves, to make their children know the happiness they had missed. They had not needed to teach each other what they saw, what they guessed, what moved them with pity and hope, and there were transitions enough safely skipped in the simple conversation I have preserved. But what Mrs. Tregent was ready to do for him filled Maurice Glanvil, for days after this, with an even greater wonder, and it seemed to him that not till then had she fully shown him that she had forgiven him.

Six months, however, proved much more than sufficient for her attempt to test the plasticity of her son. Maurice Glanvil went abroad, but was nervous and restless, wandering from place to place, revisiting old scenes and old friends, reverting, with a conscious, an even amused incongruity, and yet with an effect that was momentarily soothing, to places at which he had stayed with his wife, but feeling all the while that he was really staking his child's happiness. It only half reassured him to feel that Vera would never know what poor Fanny Knocker had been condemned to know, for the daily contact was cruel from the moment the issue was uncertain; and it only half helped him to reflect that she was not so plain as Fanny, for had not Arthur Tregent given him the impression that the young man of the present was intrinsically even more difficult to please than the young man of the past? The letters he received from Blankley conveyed no information about Arthur beyond the fact that he was at home; only once Vera mentioned that he was "remarkably good" to her. Toward the end of November he found himself in Paris, submitting reluctantly to social accidents which put off from day to day his return to London, when, one morning in the Rue de Rivoli, he had to stop short to permit the passage of a vehicle which had emerged from the court of an hotel. It was an open cab—the day was mild and bright—with a small quantity of neat, leathery luggage, which Maurice vaguely recognised as English, stowed in the place beside the driver—luggage from which his eyes shifted straight to the occupant of the carriage, a young man with his face turned to the allurements of travel and the urbanity of farewell to bowing waiters still visible in it. The young man was so bright and so on his way, as it were, that Maurice, standing there to make room for him, felt for the instant that he too had taken a tip. The feeling became acute as he recognised that this humiliating obligation was to no less a person than Arthur Tregent. It was Arthur who was so much on his way—it was Arthur who was catching a train. He noticed his mother's friend as the cab passed into the street, and, with a quick demonstration, caused the driver to pull up. He jumped out, and under the arcade the two men met with every appearance of cordiality, but with conscious confusion. Each of them coloured perceptibly, and Maurice was angry with himself for blushing before a boy. Long afterwards he remembered how cold, and even how hard, was the handsome clearness of the young eyes that met his own in an artificial smile.

"You here? I thought you were at Blankley."

"I left Blankley yesterday; I'm on my way to Spain."

"To Spain? How charming!"

"To join a friend there—just for a month or two."

"Interesting country—well worth seeing. Your mother's all right?"

"Oh, yes, all right. And Miss Glanvil——" Arthur Tregent went on, cheerfully.

"Vera's all right?" interrupted Maurice, with a still gayer tone.

"Everyone, everything's all right!" Arthur laughed.

"Well, I mustn't keep you. Bon voyage!"

Maurice Glanvil, after the young man had driven on, flattered himself that in this brief interview he had suppressed every indication of surprise; but that evening he crossed the Channel, and on the morrow he went down to Blankley. "To Spain—to Spain!" the words kept repeating themselves in his ears. He, when he had taken flight in a similar conjunction, had only got, for the time, as far as Boulogne; and he was reminded afresh of the progress of the species. When he was introduced into the drawing-room at Blankley—a chintzy, flowery, friendly expanse—Mrs. Tregent rose before him alone and offered him a face that she had never shown before. She was white and she looked scared; she faltered in her movement to meet him.

"I met Arthur in Paris, so I thought I might come."

Oh, yes; there was pain in her face, and a kind of fear of him that frightened him, but their hands found each other's hands while she replied: "He went off—I didn't know it."

"But you had a letter the next morning," Maurice said.

She stared. "How did you know that?"

"Who should know better than I? He wrote from London, explaining."

"I did what I could—I believed in it!" said Mrs Tregent. "He was charming, for a while."

"But he broke down. She's too short, eh?" Maurice asked.

"Don't laugh; she's ill."

"What's the matter with her?"

Mrs. Tregent gave the visitor a look in which there was almost a reproach for the question. "She has had a chill; she's in bed. You must see her."

She took him upstairs and he saw his child. He remembered what his mother had told him of the grievous illness of Fanny Knocker. Poor little Vera lay there in the flush of a feverish cold which had come on the evening before. She grew worse from the effect of a complication, and for three days he was anxious about her; but even more than with his alarm he held his breath before the distress, the disappointment, the humility of his old friend. Up to this hour he had not fully measured the strength of her desire to do something for him, or the intensity of passion with which she had wished to do it in the particular way that had now broken down. She had counted on her influence with her son, on his affection and on the maternal art, and there was anguish in her compunction for her failure, for her false estimate of the possible. Maurice Glanvil reminded her in vain of the consoling fact that Vera had known nothing of any plan, and he guessed indeed the reason why this theory had no comfort. No one could be better aware than Fanny Tregent of how much girls knew who knew nothing. It was doubtless this same sad wisdom that kept her sombre when he expressed a confidence that his child would promptly recover. She herself had had a terrible fight—and yet with the physical victory, had she recovered? Her apprehension for Vera was justified, for the poor girl was destined finally to forfeit even the physical victory. She got better, she got up, she quitted Blankley, she quitted England with her father, but her health had failed and a year later it gave way. Overtaken in Rome by a second illness, she succumbed; unlike Fanny Knocker she was never to have her revenge.

LORD BEAUPRÉ

I

Some reference had been made to Northerley, which was within an easy drive, and Firminger described how he had dined there the night before and had found a lot of people. Mrs. Ashbury, one of the two visitors, inquired who these people might be, and he mentioned half-a-dozen names, among which was that of young Raddle, which had been a good deal on people's lips, and even in the newspapers, on the occasion, still recent, of his stepping into the fortune, exceptionally vast even as the product of a patent-glue, left him by a father whose ugly name on all the vacant spaces of the world had exasperated generations of men.

"Oh, is he there?" asked Mrs. Ashbury, in a tone which might have been taken as a vocal rendering of the act of pricking up one's ears. She didn't hand on the information to her daughter, who was talking—if a beauty of so few phrases could have been said to talk—with Mary Gosselin, but in the course of a few moments she put down her teacup with a failure of suavity and, getting up, gave the girl a poke with her parasol. "Come, Maud, we must be stirring."

"You pay us a very short visit," said Mrs. Gosselin, intensely demure over the fine web of her knitting. Mrs. Ashbury looked hard for an instant into her bland eyes, then she gave poor Maud another poke. She alluded to a reason and expressed regrets; but she got her daughter into motion, and Guy Firminger passed through the garden with the two ladies to put them into their carriage. Mrs. Ashbury protested particularly against any further escort. While he was absent the other parent and child, sitting together on their pretty lawn in the yellow light of the August afternoon, talked of the frightful way Maud Ashbury had "gone off," and of something else as to which there was more to say when their third visitor came back.

"Don't think me grossly inquisitive if I ask you where they told the coachman to drive," said Mary Gosselin as the young man dropped, near her, into a low wicker chair, stretching his long legs as if he had been one of the family.

Firminger stared. "Upon my word I didn't particularly notice, but I think the old lady said 'Home'."

"There, mamma dear!" the girl exclaimed triumphantly.

But Mrs. Gosselin only knitted on, persisting in profundity. She replied that "Home" was a feint, that Mrs. Ashbury would already have given another order, and that it was her wish to hurry off to Northerley that had made her keep them from going with her to the carriage, in which they would have seen her take a suspected direction. Mary explained to Guy Firminger that her mother had perceived poor Mrs. Ashbury to be frantic to reach the house at which she had heard that Mr. Raddle was staying. The young man stared again and wanted to know what she desired to do with Mr. Raddle. Mary replied that her mother would tell him what Mrs. Ashbury desired to do with poor Maud.

"What all Christian mothers desire," said Mrs. Gosselin. "Only she doesn't know how."

"To marry the dear child to Mr. Raddle," Mary added, smiling.

Firminger's vagueness expanded with the subject. "Do you mean you want to marry *your* dear child to that little cad?" he asked of the elder lady.

"I speak of the general duty—not of the particular case," said Mrs. Gosselin.

"Mamma *does* know how," Mary went on.

"Then why ain't you married?"

"Because we're not acting, like the Ashburys, with injudicious precipitation. Is that correct?" the girl demanded, laughing, of her mother.

"Laugh at me, my dear, as much as you like—it's very lucky you've got me," Mrs. Gosselin declared.

"She means I can't manage for myself," said Mary to the visitor.

"What nonsense you talk!" Mrs. Gosselin murmured, counting stitches.

"I can't, mamma, I can't; I admit it," Mary continued.

"But injudicious precipitation and—what's the other thing?—creeping prudence, seem to come out in very much the same place," the young man objected.

"Do you mean since I too wither on the tree?"

"It only comes back to saying how hard it is nowadays to marry one's daughters," said the lucid Mrs. Gosselin, saving Firminger, however, the trouble of an ingenious answer. "I don't contend that, at the best, it's easy."

But Guy Firminger would not have struck you as capable of much conversational effort as he lounged there in the summer softness, with ironic familiarities, like one of the old friends who rarely deviate into sincerity. He was a robust but loose-limbed young man, with a well-shaped head and a face smooth, fair and kind. He was in knickerbockers, and his clothes, which had seen service, were composed of articles that didn't match. His laced boots were dusty—he had evidently walked a certain distance; an indication confirmed by the lingering, sociable way in which, in his basket-seat, he tilted himself towards Mary Gosselin. It pointed to a pleasant reason for a long walk. This young lady, of five-and-twenty, had black hair and blue eyes; a combination often associated with the effect of beauty. The beauty in this case, however, was dim and latent, not vulgarly obvious; and if her height and slenderness gave that impression of length of line which, as we know, is the fashion, Mary Gosselin had on the other hand too much expression to be generally admired. Every one thought her intellectual; a few of the most simple-minded even thought her plain. What Guy Firminger thought—or rather what he took for granted, for he was not built up on depths of reflection—will probably appear from this narrative.

"Yes indeed; things have come to a pass that's awful for *us*" the girl announced.

"For *us*, you mean," said Firminger. "We're hunted like the ostrich; we're trapped and stalked and run to earth. We go in fear—I assure you we do."

"Are *you* hunted, Guy?" Mrs. Gosselin asked with an inflection of her own.

"Yes, Mrs. Gosselin, even *moi qui vous parle*, the ordinary male of commerce, inconceivable as it may appear. I know something about it."

"And of whom do you go in fear?" Mary Gosselin took up an uncut book and a paper-knife which she had laid down on the advent of the other visitors.

"My dear child, of Diana and her nymphs, of the spinster at large. She's always out with her rifle. And it isn't only that; you know there's always a second gun, a walking arsenal, at her heels. I forget, for the moment, who Diana's mother was, and the genealogy of the nymphs; but not only do the old ladies know the younger ones are out, they distinctly go *with* them."

"Who was Diana's mother, my dear?" Mrs. Gosselin inquired of her daughter.

"She was a beautiful old lady with pink ribbons in her cap and a genius for knitting," the girl replied, cutting her book.

"Oh, I'm not speaking of you two dears; you're not like anyone else; you're an immense comfort," said Guy Firminger. "But they've reduced it to a science, and I assure you that if one were any one in particular, if one were not protected by one's obscurity, one's life would be a burden. Upon my honour one wouldn't escape. I've seen it, I've watched them. Look at poor Beaupré—look at little Raddle over there. I object to him, but I bleed for him."

"Lord Beaupré won't marry again," said Mrs. Gosselin with an air of conviction.

"So much the worse for him!"

"Come—that's a concession to our charms!" Mary laughed.

But the ruthless young man explained away his concession. "I mean that to be married's the only protection—or else to be engaged."

"To be permanently engaged,—wouldn't that do?" Mary Gosselin asked.

"Beautifully—I would try it if I were a *parti*."

"And how's the little boy?" Mrs. Gosselin presently inquired.

"What little boy?"

"Your little cousin—Lord Beaupré's child: isn't it a boy?"

"Oh, poor little beggar, he isn't up to much. He was awfully cut up by scarlet fever."

"You're not the rose indeed, but you're tolerably near it," the elder lady presently continued.

"What do you call near it? Not even in the same garden—not in any garden at all, alas!"

"There are three lives—but after all!"

"Dear lady, don't be homicidal!"

"What do you call the 'rose'?" Mary asked of her mother.

"The title," said Mrs. Gosselin, promptly but softly.

Something in her tone made Firminger laugh aloud. "You don't mention the property."

"Oh, I mean the whole thing."

"Is the property very large?" said Mary Gosselin.

"Fifty thousand a year," her mother responded; at which the young man laughed out again.

"Take care, mamma, or we shall be thought to be out with our guns!" the girl interposed; a recommendation that drew from Guy Firminger the just remark that there would be time enough for this when his prospects should be worth speaking of. He leaned over to pick up his hat and stick, as if it were his time to go, but he didn't go for another quarter of an hour, and during these minutes his prospects received some frank consideration. He was Lord Beaupré's first cousin, and the three intervening lives were his lordship's own, that of his little sickly son, and that of his uncle the Major, who was also Guy's uncle and with whom the young man was at present staying. It was from homely Trist, the Major's house, that he had walked over to Mrs. Gosselin's. Frank Firminger, who had married in youth a woman with something of her own and eventually left the army, had nothing but girls, but he was only of middle age and might possibly still have a son. At any rate his life was a very good one. Beaupré might marry again, and, marry or not, he was barely thirty-three and might live to a great age. The child moreover, poor little devil, would doubtless, with the growing consciousness of an incentive (there was none like feeling you were in people's way), develop a capacity for duration; so that altogether Guy professed himself, with the best will in the world, unable to take a rosy view of the disappearance of obstacles. He treated the subject with a jocularity that, in view of the remoteness of his chance, was not wholly tasteless, and the discussion, between old friends and in the light of this extravagance, was less crude than perhaps it sounds. The young man quite declined to see any latent brilliancy in his future. They had all been lashing him up, his poor dear mother, his uncle Frank, and Beaupré as well, to make that future political; but even if he should get in (he was nursing—oh, so languidly!—a possible opening), it would only be into the shallow edge of the stream. He would stand there like a tall idiot with the water up to his ankles. He didn't know how to swim—in that element; he didn't know how to do anything.

"I think you're very perverse, my dear," said Mrs. Gosselin. "I'm sure you have great dispositions."

"For what—except for sitting here and talking with you and Mary? I revel in this sort of thing, but I scarcely like anything else."

"You'd do very well if you weren't so lazy," Mary said. "I believe you're the very laziest person in the world."

"So do I—the very laziest in the world," the young man contentedly replied. "But how can I regret it, when it keeps me so quiet, when (I might even say) it makes me so amiable?"

"You'll have, one of these days, to get over your quietness, and perhaps even a little over your amiability," Mrs. Gosselin sagaciously stated.

"I devoutly hope not."

"You'll have to perform the duties of your position."

"Do you mean keep my stump of a broom in order and my crossing irreproachable?"

"You may say what you like; you will be a *parti*," Mrs. Gosselin continued.

"Well, then, if the worst comes to the worst I shall do what I said just now: I shall get some good plausible girl to see me through."

"The proper way to 'get' her will be to marry her. After you're married you won't be a *parti*."

"Dear mamma, he'll think you're already levelling your rifle!" Mary Gosselin laughingly wailed.

Guy Firminger looked at her a moment. "I say, Mary, wouldn't *you* do?"

"For the good plausible girl? Should I be plausible enough?"

"Surely—what could be more natural? Everything would seem to contribute to the suitability of our alliance. I should be known to have known you for years—from childhood's sunny hour; I should be known to have bullied you, and even to have been bullied *by* you, in the period of pinafores. My relations from a tender age with your brother, which led to our schoolroom romps in holidays and to the happy footing on which your mother has always been so good as to receive me here, would add to all the presumptions of intimacy. People would accept such a conclusion as inevitable."

"Among all your reasons you don't mention the young lady's attractions," said Mary Gosselin.

Firminger stared a moment, his clear eye lighted by his happy thought. "I don't mention the young man's. They would be so obvious, on one side and the other, as to be taken for granted."

"And is it your idea that one should pretend to be engaged to you all one's life?"

"Oh no, simply till I should have had time to look round. I'm determined not to be hustled and bewildered into matrimony—to be dragged to the shambles before I know where I am. With such an arrangement as the one I speak of I should be able to take my time, to keep my head, to make my choice."

"And how would the young lady make hers?"

"How do you mean, hers?"

"The selfishness of men is something exquisite. Suppose the young lady—if it's conceivable that you should find one idiotic enough to be a party to such a transaction—suppose the poor girl herself should happen to wish to be *really* engaged?"

Guy Firminger thought a moment, with his slow but not stupid smile. "Do you mean to *me*?"

"To you—or to some one else."

"Oh, if she'd give me notice I'd let her off."

"Let her off till you could find a substitute?"

"Yes—but I confess it would be a great inconvenience. People wouldn't take the second one so seriously."

"She would have to make a sacrifice; she would have to wait till you should know where you were," Mrs. Gosselin suggested.

"Yes, but where would *her* advantage come in?" Mary persisted.

"Only in the pleasure of charity; the moral satisfaction of doing a fellow a good turn," said Firminger.

"You must think people are keen to oblige you!"

"Ah, but surely I could count on *you*, couldn't I?" the young man asked.

Mary had finished cutting her book; she got up and flung it down on the tea-table. "What a preposterous conversation!" she exclaimed with force, tossing the words from her as she tossed her book; and, looking round her vaguely a moment, without meeting Guy Firminger's eye, she walked away to the house.

Firminger sat watching her; then he said serenely to her mother: "Why has our Mary left us?"

"She has gone to get something, I suppose."

"What has she gone to get?"

"A little stick to beat you perhaps."

"You don't mean I've been objectionable?"

"Dear, no—I'm joking. One thing is very certain," pursued Mrs. Gosselin; "that you ought to work—to try to get on exactly as if nothing could ever happen. Oughtn't you?" She threw off the question mechanically as her visitor continued silent.

"I'm sure she doesn't like it!" he exclaimed, without heeding her appeal.

"Doesn't like what?"

"My free play of mind. It's perhaps too much in the key of our old romps."

"You're very clever; she always likes *that*," said Mrs. Gosselin. "You ought to go in for something serious, for something honourable," she continued, "just as much as if you had nothing at all to look to."

"Words of wisdom, dear Mrs. Gosselin," Firminger replied, rising slowly from his relaxed attitude. "But what *have* I to look to."

She raised her mild, deep eyes to him as he stood before her—she might have been a fairy godmother. "Everything!"

"But you know I can't poison them!"

"That won't be necessary."

He looked at her an instant; then with a laugh: "One might think *you* would undertake it!"

"I almost would—for *you*. Good-bye."

"Take care,—if they *should* be carried off!" But Mrs. Gosselin only repeated her good-bye, and the young man departed before Mary had come back.

II

Nearly two years after Guy Firminger had spent that friendly hour in Mrs. Gosselin's little garden in Hampshire this far-seeing woman was enabled (by the return of her son, who at New York, in an English bank, occupied a position they all rejoiced over—to such great things might it duly lead), to resume possession, for the season, of the little London house which her husband had left her to inhabit, but which her native thrift, in determining her to let it for a term, had converted into a source of income. Hugh Gosselin, who was thirty years old and at twenty-three, before his father's death, had been dispatched to America to exert himself, was understood to be doing very well—so well that his devotion to the interests of his employers had been rewarded, for the first time, with a real holiday. He was to remain in England from May to August, undertaking, as he said, to make it all right if during this time his mother should occupy (to contribute to his entertainment), the habitation in Chester Street. He was a small, preoccupied young man, with a sharpness as acquired as a new hat; he struck his mother and sister as intensely American. For the first few days after his arrival they were startled by his intonations, though they admitted that they had had an escape when he reminded them that he might have brought with him an accent embodied in a wife.

"When you do take one," said Mrs. Gosselin, who regarded such an accident, over there, as inevitable, "you must charge her high for it."

It was not with this question, however, that the little family in Chester Street was mainly engaged, but with the last incident in the extraordinary succession of events which, like a chapter of romance, had in the course of a few months converted their vague and impecunious friend into a personage envied and honoured. It was as if a blight had been cast on all Guy Firminger's hindrances. On the day Hugh Gosselin sailed from New York the delicate little boy at Bosco had succumbed to an attack of diphtheria. His father had died of typhoid the previous winter at Naples; his uncle, a few weeks later, had had a fatal accident in the hunting-field. So strangely, so rapidly had the situation cleared up, had his fate and theirs worked for him. Guy had opened his eyes one morning to an earldom which carried with it a fortune not alone nominally but really great. Mrs. Gosselin and Mary had not written to him, but they knew he was at Bosco; he had remained there after the funeral of the late little lord. Mrs. Gosselin, who heard everything, had heard somehow that he was behaving with the greatest consideration, giving the guardians, the trustees, whatever they were called, plenty of time to do everything. Everything was comparatively simple; in the absence of collaterals there were so few other people concerned. The principal relatives were poor Frank Firminger's widow and her girls, who had seen themselves so near to new honours and comforts. Probably the girls would expect their cousin Guy to marry one of them, and think it the least he could decently do; a view the young man himself (if he were very magnanimous) might possibly embrace. The question would be whether he would be very magnanimous. These young ladies exhausted in their three persons the numerous varieties of plainness. On the other hand Guy Firminger—or Lord Beaupré, as one would have to begin to call him now—was unmistakably kind. Mrs. Gosselin appealed to her son as to whether their noble friend were not unmistakably kind.

"Of course I've known him always, and that time he came out to America—when was it? four years ago—I saw him every day. I like him awfully and all that, but since you push me, you know," said Hugh Gosselin, "I'm bound to say that the first thing to mention in any description of him would be—if you wanted to be quite correct—that he's unmistakably selfish."

"I see—I see," Mrs. Gosselin unblushingly replied. "Of course I know what you mean," she added in a moment. "But is he any more so than any one else? Every one's unmistakably selfish."

"Every one but you and Mary," said the young man.

"And *you*, dear!" his mother smiled. "But a person may be kind, you know—mayn't he?—at the same time that he *is* selfish. There are different sorts."

"Different sorts of kindness?" Hugh Gosselin asked with a laugh; and the inquiry undertaken by his mother occupied them for the moment, demanding a subtlety of treatment from which they were not conscious of shrinking, of which rather they had an idea that they were perhaps exceptionally capable. They came back to the temperate view that Guy would never put himself out, would probably never do anything great, but might show himself all the same a delightful member of society. Yes, he was probably selfish, like other people; but unlike most of them he was, somehow, amiably, attachingly, sociably, almost lovably selfish. Without doing anything great he would yet be a great success—a big, pleasant, gossiping, lounging and, in its way doubtless very splendid, presence. He would have no ambition, and it was ambition that made selfishness ugly. Hugh and his mother were sure of this last point until Mary, before whom the discussion, when it reached this stage, happened to be carried on, checked them by asking whether that, on the contrary, were not just what was supposed to make it fine.

"Oh, he only wants to be comfortable," said her brother; "but he *does* want it!"

"There'll be a tremendous rush for him," Mrs. Gosselin prophesied to her son.

"Oh, he'll never marry. It will be too much trouble."

"It's done here without any trouble—for the men. One sees how long you've been out of the country."

"There was a girl in New York whom he might have married—he really liked her. But he wouldn't turn round for her."

"Perhaps she wouldn't turn round for *him*," said Mary.

"I daresay she'll turn round *now*," Mrs. Gosselin rejoined; on which Hugh mentioned that there was nothing to be feared from her, all her revolutions had been accomplished. He added that nothing would make any difference—so intimate was his conviction that Beaupré would preserve his independence.

"Then I think he's not so selfish as you say," Mary declared; "or at any rate one will never know whether he is. Isn't married life the great chance to show it?"

"Your father never showed it," said Mrs. Gosselin; and as her children were silent in presence of this tribute to the departed she added, smiling: "Perhaps you think that *I* did!" They embraced her, to indicate what they thought, and the conversation ended, when she had remarked that Lord Beaupré was a man who would be perfectly easy to manage *after* marriage, with Hugh's exclaiming that this was doubtless exactly why he wished to keep out of it.

Such was evidently his wish, as they were able to judge in Chester Street when he came up to town. He appeared there oftener than was to have been expected, not taking himself in his new character at all too seriously to find stray half-hours for old friends. It was plain that he was going to do just as he liked, that he was not a bit excited or uplifted by his change of fortune. Mary Gosselin observed that he had no imagination—she even reproached him with the deficiency to his face; an incident which showed indeed how little seriously *she* took him. He had no idea of playing a part, and yet he would have been clever enough. He wasn't even systematic about being simple; his simplicity was a series of accidents and indifferences. Never was a man more conscientiously superficial. There were matters on which he valued Mrs. Gosselin's judgment and asked her advice—without, as usually appeared later, ever taking it; such questions, mainly, as the claims of a predecessor's servants, and those, in respect to social intercourse, of the clergyman's family. He didn't like his parson—what was a fellow to do when he didn't like his parson? What he did like was to talk with Hugh about American investments, and it was amusing to Hugh, though he tried not to show his amusement, to find himself looking at Guy Firminger in the light of capital. To Mary he addressed from the first the oddest snatches of confidential discourse, rendered in fact, however, by the levity of his tone, considerably less confidential than in intention. He had something to tell her that he joked about, yet without admitting that it was any less important for being laughable. It was neither more nor less than that Charlotte Firminger, the eldest of his late uncle's four girls, had designated to him in the clearest manner the person she considered he ought to marry. She appealed to his sense of justice, she spoke and wrote, or at any rate she looked and moved, she sighed and sang, in the name of common honesty. He had had four letters from her that week, and to his knowledge there were a series of people in London, people she could bully, whom she had got to promise to take her in for the season. She was going to be on the spot, she was going to follow him up. He took his stand on common honesty, but he had a mortal horror of Charlotte. At the same time, when a girl had a jaw like that and had marked you—really *marked* you, mind, you felt your safety oozing away. He had given them during the past three months, all those terrible girls, every sort of present that Bond Street could supply: but these demonstrations had only been held to constitute another pledge. Therefore what was a fellow to do? Besides, there were other portents; the air was thick with them, as the sky over battlefields was darkened by the flight of vultures. They were flocking, the birds of prey, from every quarter, and every girl in England, by Jove! was going to be thrown at his head. What had he done to deserve such a fate? He wanted to stop in England and see all sorts of things through; but how could he stand there and face such a charge? Yet what good would it do to bolt? Wherever he should go there would be fifty of them there first. On his honour he could say that he didn't deserve it; he had never, to his own sense, been a flirt, such a flirt at least as to have given anyone a handle. He appealed candidly to Mary Gosselin to know whether his past conduct justified such penalties. "*Have* I been a flirt?—have I given anyone a handle?" he inquired with pathetic intensity.

She met his appeal by declaring that he had been awful, committing himself right and left; and this manner of treating his affliction contributed to the sarcastic publicity (as regarded the little house in Chester Street) which presently became its natural element. Lord Beaupré's comical and yet thoroughly grounded view of his danger was soon a frequent theme among the Gosselins, who however had their own reasons for not communicating the alarm. They had no motive for concealing their interest in their old friend, but their allusions to him among their other friends may be said on the whole to have been studied. His state of mind recalled of course to Mary and her mother the queer talk about his prospects that they had had, in the country, that afternoon on which Mrs. Gosselin had been so strangely prophetic (she confessed that she had had a flash of divination: the future had been mysteriously revealed to her), and poor Guy too had seen himself quite as he was to be. He had seen his nervousness, under inevitable pressure, deepen to a panic, and he now, in intimate hours, made no attempt to disguise that a panic had become his portion. It was a fixed idea with him that he should fall a victim to woven toils, be caught in a trap constructed with superior science. The science evolved in an enterprising age by this branch of industry, the manufacture of the trap matrimonial, he had terrible anecdotes to illustrate; and what had he on his lips but a scientific term when he declared, as he perpetually did, that it was his fate to be hypnotised?

Mary Gosselin reminded him, they each in turn reminded him that his safeguard was to fall in love: were he once to put himself under that protection all the mothers and maids in Mayfair would not prevail against him. He replied that this was just the impossibility; it took leisure and calmness and opportunity and a free mind to fall in love, and never was a man less open to such experiences. He was literally fighting his way. He reminded the girl of his old fancy for pretending already to have disposed of his hand if he could put that hand on a young person who should like him well enough to be willing to participate in the fraud. She would have to place herself in rather a false position of course—have to take a certain amount of trouble; but there would after all be a good deal of fun in it (there was always fun in duping the world,) between the pair themselves, the two happy comedians.

"Why should they both be happy?" Mary Gosselin asked. "I understand why you should; but, frankly, I don't quite grasp the reason of *her* pleasure."

Lord Beaupré, with his sunny human eyes, thought a moment. "Why, for the lark, as they say, and that sort of thing. I should be awfully nice to her."

"She would require indeed to be in want of recreation!"

"Ah, but I should want a good sort—a quiet, reasonable one, you know!" he somewhat eagerly interposed.

"You're too delightful!" Mary Gosselin exclaimed, continuing to laugh. He thanked her for this appreciation, and she returned to her point—that she didn't really see the advantage his accomplice could hope to enjoy as her compensation for extreme disturbance.

Guy Firminger stared. "But what extreme disturbance?"

"Why, it would take a lot of time; it might become intolerable."

"You mean I ought to pay her—to hire her for the season?"

Mary Gosselin considered him a moment. "Wouldn't marriage come cheaper at once?" she asked with a quieter smile.

"You *are* chaffing me!" he sighed forgivingly. "Of course she would have to be good-natured enough to pity me."

"Pity's akin to love. If she were good-natured enough to want so to help you she'd be good-natured enough to want to marry you. That would be *her* idea of help."

"Would it be *yours*?" Lord Beaupré asked rather eagerly.

"You're too absurd! You must sail your own boat!" the girl answered, turning away.

That evening at dinner she stated to her companions that she had never seen a fatuity so dense, so serene, so preposterous as his lordship's.

"Fatuity, my dear! what do you mean?" her mother inquired.

"Oh, mamma, you know perfectly." Mary Gosselin spoke with a certain impatience.

"If you mean he's conceited I'm bound to say I don't agree with you," her brother observed. "He's too indifferent to everyone's opinion for that."

"He's not vain, he's not proud, he's not pompous," said Mrs. Gosselin.

Mary was silent a moment. "He takes more things for granted than anyone I ever saw."

"What sort of things?"

"Well, one's interest in his affairs."

"With old friends surely a gentleman may."

"Of course," said Hugh Gosselin, "old friends have in turn the right to take for granted a corresponding interest on *his* part."

"Well, who could be nicer to us than he is or come to see us oftener?" his mother asked.

"He comes exactly for the purpose I speak of—to talk about himself," said Mary.

"There are thousands of girls who would be delighted with his talk," Mrs. Gosselin returned.

"We agreed long ago that he's intensely selfish," the girl went on; "and if I speak of it to-day it's not because that in itself is anything of a novelty. What I'm freshly struck with is simply that he more shamelessly shows it."

"He shows it, exactly," said Hugh; "he shows all there is. There it is, on the surface; there are not depths of it underneath."

"He's not hard," Mrs. Gosselin contended; "he's not impervious."

"Do you mean he's soft?" Mary asked.

"I mean he's yielding." And Mrs. Gosselin, with considerable expression, looked across at her daughter. She added, before they rose from dinner, that poor Beaupré had plenty of difficulties and that she thought, for her part, they ought in common loyalty to do what they could to assist him.

For a week nothing more passed between the two ladies on the subject of their noble friend, and in the course of this week they had the amusement of receiving in Chester Street a member of Hugh's American circle, Mr. Bolton-Brown, a young man from New York. He was a person engaged in large affairs, for whom Hugh Gosselin professed the highest regard, from whom in New York he had received much hospitality, and for whose advent he had from the first prepared his companions. Mrs. Gosselin begged the amiable stranger to stay with them, and if she failed to overcome his hesitation it was because his hotel was near at hand and he should be able to see them often. It became evident that he would do so, and, to the two ladies, as the days went by, equally evident that no objection to such a relation was likely to arise. Mr. Bolton-Brown was delightfully fresh; the most usual expressions acquired on his lips a wellnigh comical novelty, the most superficial sentiments, in the look with which he accompanied them, a really touching sincerity. He was unmarried and good-looking, clever and natural, and if he was not very rich was at least very free-handed. He literally strewed the path of the ladies in Chester Street with flowers, he choked them with French confectionery. Hugh, however, who was often rather mysterious on monetary questions, placed in a light sufficiently clear the fact that his friend had in Wall Street (they knew all about Wall Street), improved each shining hour. They introduced him to Lord Beaupré, who thought him "tremendous fun," as Hugh said, and who immediately declared that the four must spend a Sunday at Bosco a week or two later. The date of this visit was fixed—Mrs. Gosselin had uttered a comprehensive acceptance; but after Guy Firminger had taken leave of them (this had been his first appearance since the odd conversation with Mary), our young lady confided to her mother that she should not be able to join the little party. She expressed the conviction that it would be all that was essential if Mrs. Gosselin should go with the two others. On being pressed to communicate the reason of this aloofness Mary was able to give no better one than that she never had cared for Bosco.

"What makes you hate him so?" her mother presently broke out in a tone which brought the red to the girl's cheek. Mary denied that she entertained for Lord Beaupré any sentiment so intense; to which Mrs. Gosselin rejoined with some sternness and, no doubt, considerable wisdom: "Look out what you do then, or you'll be thought by everyone to be in love with him!"

III

I know not whether it was this danger—that of appearing to be moved to extremes—that weighed with Mary Gosselin; at any rate when the day arrived she had decided to be perfectly colourless and take her share of Lord Beaupré's hospitality. On perceiving that the house, when with her companions she reached it, was full of visitors, she consoled herself with the sense that such a share would be of the smallest. She even wondered whether its smallness might not be caused in some degree by the sufficiently startling presence, in this stronghold of the single life, of Maud Ashbury and her mother. It was true that during the Saturday evening she never saw their host address an observation to them; but she was struck, as she had been struck before, with the girl's cold and magnificent beauty. It was very well to say she had "gone off"; she was still handsomer than anyone else. She had failed in everything she had tried; the campaign undertaken with so much energy against young Raddle had been conspicuously disastrous. Young Raddle had married his grandmother, or a person who might have filled such an office, and Maud was a year older, a year more disappointed and a year more ridiculous. Nevertheless one could scarcely believe that a creature with such advantages would always fail, though indeed the poor girl was stupid enough to be a warning. Perhaps it would be at Bosco, or with the master of Bosco, that fate had appointed her to succeed. Except Mary herself she was the only young unmarried woman on the scene, and Mary glowed with the generous sense of not being a competitor. She felt as much out of the question as the blooming wives, the heavy matrons, who formed the rest of the female contingent. Before the evening closed, however, her host, who, she saw, was delightful in his own house, mentioned to her that he had a couple of guests who had not been invited.

"Not invited?"

"They drove up to my door as they might have done to an inn. They asked for rooms and complained of those that were given them. Don't pretend not to know who they are."

"Do you mean the Ashburys? How amusing!"

"Don't laugh; it freezes my blood."

"Do you really mean you're afraid of them?"

"I tremble like a leaf. Some monstrous ineluctable fate seems to look at me out of their eyes."

"That's because you secretly admire Maud. How can you help it? She's extremely good-looking, and if you get rid of her mother she'll become a very nice girl."

"It's an odious thing, no doubt, to say about a young person under one's own roof, but I don't think I ever saw any one who happened to be less to my taste," said Guy Firminger. "I don't know why I don't turn them out even now."

Mary persisted in sarcasm. "Perhaps you can make her have a worse time by letting her stay."

"*Please* don't laugh," her interlocutor repeated. "Such a fact as I have mentioned to you seems to me to speak volumes—to show you what my life is."

"Oh, your life, your life!" Mary Gosselin murmured, with her mocking note.

"Don't you agree that at such a rate it may easily become impossible?"

"Many people would change with you. I don't see what there is for you to do but to bear your cross!"

"That's easy talk!" Lord Beaupré sighed.

"Especially from me, do you mean? How do you know I don't bear mine?"

"Yours?" he asked vaguely.

"How do you know that *I*'m not persecuted, that *my* footsteps are not dogged, that *my* life isn't a burden?"

They were walking in the old gardens, the proprietor of which, at this, stopped short. "Do you mean by fellows who want to marry you?"

His tone produced on his companion's part an irrepressible peal of hilarity; but she walked on as she exclaimed: "You speak as if there couldn't *be* such madmen!"

"Of course such a charming girl must be made up to," Guy Firminger conceded as he overtook her.

"I don't speak of it; I keep quiet about it."

"You realise then, at any rate, that it's all horrid when you don't care for them."

"I suffer in silence, because I know there are worse tribulations. It seems to me you ought to remember that," Mary continued. "Your cross is small compared with your crown. You've everything in the world that most people most desire, and I'm bound to say I think your life is made very comfortable for you. If you're oppressed by the quantity of interest and affection you inspire you ought simply to make up your mind to bear up and be cheerful under it."

Lord Beaupré received this admonition with perfect good humour; he professed himself able to do it full justice. He remarked that he would gladly give up some of his material advantages to be a little less badgered, and that he had been quite content with his former insignificance. No doubt, however, such annoyances were the essential drawbacks of ponderous promotions; one had to pay for everything. Mary was quite right to rebuke him; her own attitude, as a young woman much admired, was a lesson to his irritability. She cut this appreciation short, speaking of something else; but a few minutes later he broke out irrelevantly: "Why, if you are hunted as well as I, that dodge I proposed to you would be just the thing for us *both*!" He had evidently been reasoning it out.

Mary Gosselin was silent at first; she only paused gradually in their walk at a point where four long alleys met. In the centre of the circle, on a massive pedestal, rose in Italian bronze a florid, complicated image, so that the place made a charming old-world picture. The grounds of Bosco were stately without stiffness and full of marble terraces and misty avenues. The fountains in particular were royal. The girl had told her mother in London that she disliked this fine residence, but she now looked round her with a vague pleased sigh, holding up her glass (she had been condemned to wear one, with a long handle, since she was fifteen), to consider the weather-stained garden group. "What a perfect place of its kind!" she musingly exclaimed.

"Wouldn't it really be just the thing?" Lord Beaupré went on, with the eagerness of his idea.

"Wouldn't what be just the thing?"

"Why, the defensive alliance we've already talked of. You wanted to know the good it would do *you*. Now you see the good it would do you!"

"I don't like practical jokes," said Mary. "The remedy's worse than the disease," she added; and she began to follow one of the paths that took the direction of the house.

Poor Lord Beaupré was absurdly in love with his invention; he had all an inventor's importunity. He kept up his attempt to place his "dodge" in a favourable light, in spite of a further objection from his companion, who assured him that it was one of those contrivances which break down in practice in just the proportion in which they make a figure in theory. At last she said: "I was not sincere just now when I told you I'm worried. I'm not worried!"

"They *don't* buzz about you?" Guy Firminger asked.

She hesitated an instant. "They buzz about me; but at bottom it's flattering and I don't mind it. Now please drop the subject."

He dropped the subject, though not without congratulating her on the fact that, unlike his infirm self, she could keep her head and her temper. His infirmity found a trap laid for it before they had proceeded twenty yards, as was proved by his sudden exclamation of horror. "Good Heavens—if there isn't Lottie!"

Mary perceived, in effect, in the distance a female figure coming towards them over a stretch of lawn, and she simultaneously saw, as a gentleman passed from behind a clump of shrubbery, that it was not unattended. She recognized Charlotte Firminger, and she also distinguished the gentleman. She was moved to larger mirth at the dismay expressed by poor Firminger, but she was able to articulate: "Walking with Mr. Brown."

Lord Beaupré stopped again before they were joined by the pair. "Does *he* buzz about you?"

"Mercy, what questions you ask!" his companion exclaimed.

"Does he—*please*?" the young man repeated with odd intensity.

Mary looked at him an instant; she was puzzled by the deep annoyance that had flushed through the essential good-humour of his face. Then she saw that this annoyance had exclusive reference to poor Charlotte; so that it left her free to reply, with another laugh: "Well, yes—he does. But you know I like it!"

"I don't, then!" Before she could have asked him, even had she wished to, in what manner such a circumstance concerned him, he added with his droll agitation: "I never invited *her*, either! Don't let her get at me!"

"What can I do?" Mary demanded as the others advanced.

"Please take her away; keep her yourself! I'll take the American, I'll keep *him*," he murmured, inconsequently, as a bribe.

"But I don't object to him."

"Do you like him so much?"

"Very much indeed," the girl replied.

The reply was perhaps lost upon her interlocutor, whose eye now fixed itself gloomily on the dauntless Charlotte. As Miss Firminger came nearer he exclaimed almost loud enough for her to hear: "I think I shall *murder* her some day!"

Mary Gosselin's first impression had been that, in his panic, under the empire of that fixed idea to which he confessed himself subject, he attributed to his kinswoman machinations and aggressions of which she was incapable; an impression that might have been confirmed by this young lady's decorous placidity, her passionless eyes, her expressionless cheeks and colourless tones. She was ugly, yet she was orthodox; she was not what writers of books called intense. But after Mary, to oblige their host, had tried, successfully enough, to be crafty, had drawn her on to stroll a little in advance of the two gentlemen, she became promptly aware, by the mystical influence of propinquity, that Miss Firminger was indeed full of views, of a purpose single, simple and strong, which gave her the effect of a person carrying with a stiff, steady hand, with eyes fixed and lips compressed, a cup charged to the brim. She had driven over to lunch, driven from somewhere in the neighbourhood; she had picked up some weak woman as an escort. Mary, though she knew the neighbourhood, failed to recognize her base of operations, and, as Charlotte was not specific, ended by suspecting that, far from being entertained by friends, she had put up at an inn and hired a fly. This suspicion startled her; it gave her for the first time something of the measure of the passions engaged, and she wondered to what the insecurity complained of by Guy might lead. Charlotte, on arriving, had gone through a part of the house in quest of its master (the servants being unable to tell her where he was), and she had finally come upon Mr. Bolton-Brown, who was looking at old books in the library. He had placed himself at her service, as if he had been trained immediately to recognize in such a case his duty, and informing her that he believed Lord Beaupré to be in the grounds, had come out with her to help to find him. Lottie Firminger questioned her companion about this accommodating person; she intimated that he was rather odd but rather nice. Mary mentioned to her that Lord Beaupré thought highly of him; she believed they were going somewhere together. At this Miss Firminger turned round to look for them, but they had already disappeared, and the girl became ominously dumb.

Mary wondered afterwards what profit she could hope to derive from such proceedings; they struck her own sense, naturally, as disreputable and desperate. She was equally unable to discover the compensation they offered, in another variety, to poor Maud Ashbury, whom Lord Beaupré, the greater part of the day, neglected as conscientiously as he neglected his cousin. She asked herself if he should be blamed, and replied that the others should be blamed first. He got rid of Charlotte somehow after tea; she had to fall back to her mysterious lines. Mary knew this method would have been detestable to him—he hated to force his friendly nature; she was sorry for him and wished to lose sight of him. She wished not to be mixed up even indirectly with his tribulations, and the fevered faces of the Ashburys were particularly dreadful to her. She spent as much of the long summer afternoon as possible out of the house, which indeed on such an occasion emptied itself of most of its inmates. Mary Gosselin asked her brother to join her in a devious ramble; she might have had other society, but she was in a mood to prefer his. These two were "great chums," and they had been separated so long that they had arrears of talk to make up. They had been at Bosco more than once, and though Hugh Gosselin said that the land of the free (which he had assured his sister was even more enslaved than dear old England) made one forget there were such spots on earth, they both remembered, a couple of miles away, a little ancient church to which the walk across the fields would be the right thing. They talked of other things as they went, and among them they talked of Mr. Bolton-Brown, in regard to whom Hugh, as scantily addicted to enthusiasm as to bursts of song (he was determined not to be taken in), became, in commendation, almost lyrical. Mary asked what he had done with his paragon, and he replied that he believed him to have gone out stealthily to sketch: they might come across him. He was extraordinarily clever at water-colours, but haunted with the fear that the public practice of such an art on Sunday was viewed with disfavour in England. Mary exclaimed that this was the respectable fact, and when her brother ridiculed the idea she told him she had already noticed he had lost all sense of things at home, so that Mr. Bolton-Brown was apparently a better Englishman than he. "He is indeed—he's awfully artificial!" Hugh returned; but it must be added that in spite of this rigour their American friend, when they reached the goal of their walk, was to be perceived in an irregular attitude in the very churchyard. He was perched on an old flat tomb, with a box of colours beside him and a sketch half completed. Hugh asserted that this exercise was the only thing that Mr. Bolton-Brown really cared for, but the young man protested against the imputation in the face of an achievement so modest. He showed his sketch to Mary however, and it consoled her for not having kept up her own experiments; she never could make her trees so leafy. He had found a lovely bit on the other side of the hill, a bit he should like to come back to, and he offered to show it to his friends. They were on the point of starting with him to look at it when Hugh Gosselin, taking out his watch, remembered the hour at which he had promised to be at the house again to give his mother, who wanted a little mild exercise, his arm. His sister, at this, said she would go back with him; but Bolton-Brown interposed an earnest inquiry. Mightn't she let Hugh keep his appointment and let *him* take her over the hill and bring her home?

"Happy thought—*do* that!" said Hugh, with a crudity that showed the girl how completely he had lost his English sense. He perceived however in an instant that she was embarrassed, whereupon he went on: "My dear child, I've walked with girls so often in America that we really ought to let poor Brown walk with one in England." I know not if it was the effect of this plea or that of some further eloquence of their friend; at any rate Mary Gosselin in the course of another minute had accepted the accident of Hugh's secession, had seen him depart with an injunction to her to render it clear to poor Brown that he had made quite a monstrous request. As she went over the hill with her companion she reflected that since she had granted the request it was not in her interest to pretend she had gone out of her way. She wondered moreover whether her brother had wished to throw them together: it suddenly occurred to her that the whole incident might have been prearranged. The idea made her a little angry with Hugh; it led her however to entertain no resentment against the other party (if party Mr. Brown had been) to the transaction. He told her all the delight that certain sweet old corners of rural England excited in his mind, and she liked him for hovering near some of her own secrets.

Hugh Gosselin meanwhile, at Bosco, strolling on the terrace with his mother, who preferred walks that were as slow as conspiracies and had had much to say to him about his extraordinary indiscretion, repeated over and over (it ended by irritating her), that as he himself had been out for hours with American girls it was only fair to let their friend have a turn with an English one.

"Pay as much as you like, but don't pay with your sister!" Mrs. Gosselin replied; while Hugh submitted that it was just his sister who was required to make the payment *his*. She turned his logic to easy scorn and she waited on the terrace till she had seen the two explorers reappear. When the ladies went to dress for dinner she expressed to her daughter her extreme disapproval of such conduct, and Mary did nothing more to justify herself than to exclaim at first "Poor dear man!" and then to say "I was afraid you wouldn't like it." There were reservations in her silence that made Mrs. Gosselin uneasy, and she was glad that at dinner Mr. Bolton-Brown had to take in Mrs. Ashbury: it served him so right. This arrangement had in Mrs. Gosselin's eyes the added merit of serving Mrs. Ashbury right. She was more uneasy than ever when after dinner, in the drawing-room, she saw Mary sit for a period on the same small sofa with the culpable American. This young couple leaned back together familiarly, and their conversation had the air of being desultory without being in the least difficult. At last she quitted her place and went over to them, remarking to Mr. Bolton-Brown that she wanted him to come and talk a bit to *her*. She conducted him to another part of the room, which was vast and animated by scattered groups, and held him there very persuasively, quite maternally, till the approach of the hour at which the ladies would exchange looks and murmur good-nights. She made him talk about America, though he wanted to talk about England, and she judged that she gave him an impression of the kindest attention, though she was really thinking, in alternation, of three important things. One of these was a circumstance of which she had become conscious only just after sitting down with him—the prolonged absence of Lord Beaupré from the drawing-room; the second was the absence, equally marked (to her imagination) of Maud Ashbury; the third was a matter different altogether. "England gives one such a sense of immemorial continuity, something that drops like a plummet-line into the past," said the young American, ingeniously exerting himself while Mrs. Gosselin, rigidly contemporaneous, strayed into deserts of conjecture. Had the fact that their host was out of the room any connection with the fact that the most beautiful, even though the most suicidal, of his satellites had quitted it? Yet if poor Guy was taking a turn by starlight on the terrace with the misguided girl, what had he done with his resentment at her invasion and by what inspiration of despair had Maud achieved such a triumph? The good lady studied Mrs. Ashbury's face across the room; she decided that triumph, accompanied perhaps with a shade of nervousness, looked out of her insincere eyes. An intelligent consciousness of ridicule was at any rate less present in them than ever. While Mrs. Gosselin had her infallible finger on the pulse of the occasion one of the doors opened to readmit Lord Beaupré, who struck her as pale and who immediately approached Mrs. Ashbury with a remark evidently intended for herself alone. It led this lady to rise with a movement of dismay and, after a question or two, leave the room. Lord Beaupré left it again in her company. Mr. Bolton-Brown had also noticed the incident; his conversation languished and he asked Mrs. Gosselin if she supposed anything had happened. She turned it over a moment and then she said: "Yes, something will have happened to Miss Ashbury."

"What do you suppose? Is she ill?"

"I don't know; we shall see. They're capable of anything."

"Capable of anything?"

"I've guessed it,—she wants to have a grievance."

"A grievance?" Mr. Bolton-Brown was mystified.

"Of course you don't understand; how should you? Moreover it doesn't signify. But I'm so vexed with them (he's a very old friend of ours) that really, though I dare say I'm indiscreet, I can't speak civilly of them."

"Miss Ashbury's a wonderful type," said the young American.

This remark appeared to irritate his companion. "I see perfectly what has happened; she has made a scene."

"A scene?" Mr. Bolton-Brown was terribly out of it.

"She has tried to be injured—to provoke him, I mean, to some act of impatience, to some failure of temper, of courtesy. She has asked him if he wishes her to leave the house at midnight, and he may have answered—— But no, he wouldn't!" Mrs. Gosselin suppressed the wild supposition.

"How you read it! She looks so quiet."

"Her mother has coached her, and (I won't pretend to say *exactly* what has happened) they've done, somehow, what they wanted; they've got him to do something to them that he'll have to make up for."

"What an evolution of ingenuity!" the young man laughed.

"It often answers."

"Will it in this case?"

Mrs. Gosselin was silent a moment. "It *may*."

"Really, you think?"

"I mean it might if it weren't for something else."

"I'm too judicious to ask what that is."

"I'll tell you when we're back in town," said Mrs. Gosselin, getting up.

Lord Beaupré was restored to them, and the ladies prepared to withdraw. Before she went to bed Mrs. Gosselin asked him if there had been anything the matter with Maud; to which he replied with abysmal blankness (she had never seen him wear just that face) that he was afraid Miss Ashbury was ill. She proved in fact in the morning too unwell to return to London: a piece of news communicated to Mrs. Gosselin at breakfast.

"She'll have to stay; I can't turn her out of the house," said Guy Firminger.

"Very well; let her stay her fill!"

"I wish you would stay too," the young man went on.

"Do you mean to nurse her?"

"No, her mother must do that. I mean to keep me company."

"*You?* You're not going up?"

"I think I had better wait over to-day, or long enough to see what's the matter."

"Don't you *know* what's the matter?"

He was silent a moment. "I may have been nasty last night."

"You have compunctions? You're too good-natured."

"I dare say I hit rather wild. It will look better for me to stop over twenty-four hours."

Mrs. Gosselin fixed her eyes on a distant object. "Let no one ever say you're selfish!"

"*Does* anyone ever say it?"

"You're too generous, you're too soft, you're too foolish. But if it will give you any pleasure Mary and I will wait till to-morrow."

"And Hugh, too, won't he, and Bolton-Brown?"

"Hugh will do as he pleases. But don't keep the American."

"Why not? He's all right."

"That's why I want him to go," said Mrs. Gosselin, who could treat a matter with candour, just as she could treat it with humour, at the right moment.

The party at Bosco broke up and there was a general retreat to town. Hugh Gosselin pleaded pressing business, he accompanied the young American to London. His mother and sister came back on the morrow, and Bolton-Brown went in to see them, as he often did, at tea-time. He found Mrs. Gosselin alone in the drawing-room, and she took such a convenient occasion to mention to him, what she had withheld on the eve of their departure from Bosco, the reason why poor Maud Ashbury's frantic assault on the master of that property would be vain. He was greatly surprised, the more so that Hugh hadn't told him. Mrs. Gosselin replied that Hugh didn't know: she had not seen him all day and it had only just come out. Hugh's friend at any rate was deeply interested, and his interest took for several minutes the form of throbbing silence. At last Mrs. Gosselin heard a sound below, on which she said quickly: "That's Hugh—I'll tell him now!" She left the room with the request that their visitor would wait for Mary, who would be down in a moment. During the instants that he spent alone the visitor lurched, as if he had been on a deck in a blow, to the window, and stood there with his hands in his pockets, staring vacantly into Chester Street; then, turning away, he gave himself, with an odd ejaculation, an impatient shake which had the effect of enabling him to meet Mary Gosselin composedly enough when she came in. It took her mother apparently some time to communicate the news to Hugh, so that Bolton-Brown had a considerable margin for nervousness and hesitation before he could say to the girl, abruptly, but with an attempt at a voice properly gay: "You must let me very heartily congratulate you!"

Mary stared. "On what?"

"On your engagement."

"My engagement?"

"To Lord Beaupré."

Mary Gosselin looked strange; she coloured. "Who told you I'm engaged?"

"Your mother—just now."

"Oh!" the girl exclaimed, turning away. She went and rang the bell for fresh tea, rang it with noticeable force. But she said "Thank you very much!" before the servant came.

IV

Bolton-Brown did something that evening toward disseminating the news: he told it to the first people he met socially after leaving Chester Street; and this although he had to do himself a certain violence in speaking. He would have preferred to hold his peace; therefore if he resisted his inclination it was for an urgent purpose. This purpose was to prove to himself that he didn't mind. A perfect indifference could be for him the only result of any understanding Mary Gosselin might arrive at with anyone, and he wanted to be more and more conscious of his indifference. He was aware indeed that it required demonstration, and this was why he was almost feverishly active. He could mentally concede at least that he had been surprised, for he had suspected nothing at Bosco. When a fellow was attentive in America everyone knew it, and judged by this standard Lord Beaupré made no show: how otherwise should *he* have achieved that sweet accompanied ramble? Everything at any rate was lucid now, except perhaps a certain ambiguity in Hugh Gosselin, who on coming into the drawing-room with his mother had looked flushed and grave and had stayed only long enough to kiss Mary and go out again. There had been nothing effusive in the scene; but then there was nothing effusive in any English scene. This helped to explain why Miss Gosselin had been so blank during the minutes she spent with him before her mother came back.

He himself wanted to cultivate tranquillity, and he felt that he did so the next day in not going again to Chester Street. He went instead to the British Museum, where he sat quite like an elderly gentleman, with his hands crossed on the top of his stick and his eyes fixed on an Assyrian bull. When he came away, however, it was with the resolution to move briskly; so that he walked westward the whole length of Oxford Street and arrived at the Marble Arch. He stared for some minutes at this monument, as in the national collection he had stared at even less intelligible ones; then brushing away the apprehension that he should meet two persons riding together, he passed into the park. He didn't care a straw whom he met. He got upon the grass and made his way to the southern expanse, and when he reached the Row he dropped into a chair, rather tired, to watch the capering procession of riders. He watched it with a lustreless eye, for what he seemed mainly to extract from it was a vivification of his disappointment. He had had a hope that he should not be forced to leave London without inducing Mary Gosselin to ride with him; but that prospect failed, for what he had accomplished in the British Museum was the determination to go to Paris. He tried to think of the attractions supposed to be evoked by that name, and while he was so engaged he recognised that a gentleman on horseback, close to the barrier of the Row, was making a sign to him. The gentleman was Lord Beaupré, who had pulled up his horse and whose sign the young American lost no time in obeying. He went forward to speak to his late host, but during the instant of the transit he was able both to observe that Mary Gosselin was not in sight and to ask himself why she was not. She rode with her brother; why then didn't she ride with her future husband? It was singular at such a moment to see her future husband disporting himself alone. This personage conversed a few moments with Bolton-Brown, said it was too hot to ride, but that he ought to be mounted (*he* would give him a mount if he liked) and was on the point of turning away when his interlocutor succumbed to the temptation to put his modesty to the test.

"Good-bye, but let me congratulate you first," said Bolton-Brown.

"Congratulate me? On what?" His look, his tone were very much what Mary Gosselin's had been.

"Why, on your engagement. Haven't you heard of it?"

Lord Beaupré stared a moment while his horse shifted uneasily. Then he laughed and said: "Which of them do you mean?"

"There's only one I know anything about. To Miss Gosselin," Brown added, after a puzzled pause.

"Oh yes, I see—thanks so much!" With this, letting his horse go, Lord Beaupré broke off, while Bolton-Brown stood looking after him and saying to himself that perhaps he *didn't* know! The chapter of English oddities was long.

But on the morrow the announcement was in "The Morning Post," and that surely made it authentic. It was doubtless only superficially singular that Guy Firminger should have found himself unable to achieve a call in Chester Street until this journal had been for several hours in circulation. He appeared there just before luncheon, and the first person who received him was Mrs. Gosselin. He had always liked her, finding her infallible on the question of behaviour; but he was on this occasion more than ever struck with her ripe astuteness, her independent wisdom.

"I knew what you wanted, I knew what you needed, I knew the subject on which you had pressed her," the good lady said; "and after Sunday I found myself really haunted with your dangers. There was danger in the air at Bosco, in your own defended house; it seemed to me too monstrous. I said to myself 'We *can* help him, poor dear, and we *must*. It's the least one can do for so old and so good a friend.' I decided what to do: I simply put this other story about. In London that always answers. I knew that Mary pitied you really as much as I do, and that what she saw at Bosco had been a revelation—had at any rate brought your situation home to her. Yet of course she would be shy about saying out for herself: 'Here I am—I'll do what you want.' The thing was for me to say it *for* her; so I said it first to that chattering American. He repeated it to several others, and there you are! I just forced her hand a little, but it's all right. All she has to do is not to contradict it. It won't be any trouble and you'll be comfortable. That will be our reward!" smiled Mrs. Gosselin.

"Yes, all she has to do is not to contradict it," Lord Beaupré replied, musing a moment. "It *won't* be any trouble," he added, "and I *hope* I shall be comfortable." He thanked Mrs. Gosselin formally and liberally, and expressed all his impatience to assure Mary herself of his deep obligation to her; upon which his hostess promised to send her daughter to him on the instant: she would go and call her, so that they might be alone. Before Mrs. Gosselin left him however she touched on one or two points that had their little importance. Guy Firminger had asked for Hugh, but Hugh had gone to the City, and his mother mentioned candidly that he didn't take part in the game. She even disclosed his reason: he thought there was a want of dignity in it. Lord Beaupré stared at this and after a moment exclaimed: "Dignity? Dignity be hanged! One must save one's life!"

"Yes, but the point poor Hugh makes is that one must save it by the use of one's *own* wits, or one's *own* arms and legs. But do you know what I said to him?" Mrs. Gosselin continued.

"Something very clever, I daresay."

"That if *we* were drowning you'd be the very first to jump in. And we may fall overboard yet!" Fidgeting there with his hands in his pockets Lord Beaupré gave a laugh at this, but assured her that there was nothing in the world for which they mightn't count upon him. None the less she just permitted herself another warning, a warning, it is true, that was in his own interest, a reminder of a peril that he ought beforehand to look in the face. Wasn't there always the chance—just the bare chance—that a girl in Mary's position would, in the event, decline to let him off, decline to release him even on the day he should wish to marry? She wasn't speaking of Mary, but there were of course girls who would play him that trick. Guy Firminger considered this contingency; then he declared that it wasn't a question of 'girls,' it was simply a question of dear old Mary! If *she* should wish to hold him, so much the better: he would do anything in the world that she wanted. "Don't let us dwell on such vulgarities; but I had it on my conscience!" Mrs. Gosselin wound up.

She left him, but at the end of three minutes Mary came in, and the first thing she said was: "Before you speak a word, please understand this, that it's wholly mamma's doing. I hadn't dreamed of it, but she suddenly began to tell people."

"It was charming of her, and it's charming of you!" the visitor cried.

"It's not charming of any one, I think," said Mary Gosselin, looking at the carpet. "It's simply idiotic."

"Don't be nasty about it. It will be tremendous fun."

"I've only consented because mamma says we owe it to you," the girl went on.

"Never mind your reason—the end justifies the means. I can never thank you enough nor tell you what a weight it lifts off my shoulders. Do you know I feel the difference already?—a peace that passeth understanding!" Mary replied that this was childish; how could such a feeble fiction last? At the very best it could live but an hour, and then he would be no better off than before. It would bristle moreover with difficulties and absurdities; it would be so much more trouble than it was worth. She reminded him that so ridiculous a service had never been asked of any girl, and at this he seemed a little struck; he said: "Ah, well, if it's positively disagreeable to you we'll instantly drop the idea. But I—I thought you really liked me enough——!" She turned away impatiently, and he went on to argue imperturbably that she had always treated him in the kindest way in the world. He added that the worst was over, the start, they were off: the thing would be in all the evening papers. Wasn't it much simpler to accept it? That was all they would have to do; and all *she* would have to do would be not to gainsay it and to smile and thank people when she was congratulated. She would have to *act* a little, but that would just be part of the fun. Oh, he hadn't the shadow of a scruple about taking the world in; the world deserved it richly, and she couldn't deny that this was what she had felt for him, that she had really been moved to compassion. He grew eloquent and charged her with having recognised in his predicament a genuine motive for charity. Their little plot would last what it could—it would be a part of their amusement to *make* it last. Even if it should be but a thing of a day there would have been always so much gained. But they would be ingenious, they would find ways, they would have no end of sport.

"*You* must be ingenious; I can't," said Mary. "If people scarcely ever see us together they'll guess we're trying to humbug them."

"But they *will* see us together. We *are* together. We've been together—I mean we've seen a lot of each other—all our lives."

"Ah, not *that* way!"

"Oh, trust me to work it right!" cried the young man, whose imagination had now evidently begun to glow in the air of their pious fraud.

"You'll find it a dreadful bore," said Mary Gosselin.

"Then I'll drop it, don't you see? And *you*'ll drop it, of course, the moment *you*'ve had enough," Lord Beaupré punctually added. "But as soon as you begin to realise what a lot of good you do me you won't *want* to drop it. That is if you're what I take you for!" laughed his lordship.

If a third person had been present at this conversation—and there was nothing in it surely that might not have been spoken before a trusty listener—that person would perhaps have thought, from the immediate expression of Mary Gosselin's face, that she was on the point of exclaiming "You take me for too big a fool!" No such ungracious words in fact however passed her lips; she only said after an instant: "What reason do you propose to give, on the day you need one, for our rupture?"

Her interlocutor stared. "To you, do you mean?"

"*I* sha'n't ask you for one. I mean to other people."

"Oh, I'll tell them you're sick of me. I'll put everything on you, and you'll put everything on me."

"You *have* worked it out!" Mary exclaimed.

"Oh, I shall be intensely considerate."

"Do you call that being considerate—publicly accusing me?"

Guy Firminger stared again. "Why, isn't that the reason *you*'ll give?"

She looked at him an instant. "I won't tell you the reason I shall give."

"Oh, I shall learn it from others."

"I hope you'll like it when you do!" said Mary, with sudden gaiety; and she added frankly though kindly the hope that he might soon light upon some young person who would really meet his requirements. He replied that he shouldn't be in a hurry—that was now just the comfort; and she, as if thinking over to the end the list of arguments against his clumsy contrivance, broke out: "And of course you mustn't dream of giving me anything—any tokens or presents."

"Then it won't look natural."

"That's exactly what I say. You can't make it deceive anybody."

"I *must* give you something—something that people can see. There must be some evidence! You can simply put my offerings away after a little and give them back." But about this Mary was visibly serious; she declared that she wouldn't touch anything that came from his hand, and she spoke in such a tone that he coloured a little and hastened to say: "Oh, all right, I shall be thoroughly careful!" This appeared to complete their understanding; so that after it was settled that for the deluded world they were engaged, there was obviously nothing for him to do but to go. He therefore shook hands with her very gratefully and departed.

V

He was able promptly to assure his accomplice that their little plot was working to a charm; it already made such a difference for the better. Only a week had elapsed, but he felt quite another man; his life was no longer spent in springing to arms and he had ceased to sleep in his boots. The ghost of his great fear was laid, he could follow out his inclinations and attend to his neglected affairs. The news had been a bomb in the enemy's camp, and there were plenty of blank faces to testify to the confusion it had wrought. Every one was "sold" and every one made haste to clap him on the back. Lottie Firminger only had written in terms of which no notice could be taken, though of course he expected, every time he came in, to find her waiting in his hall. Her mother was coming up to town and he should have the family at his ears; but, taking them as a single body, he could manage them, and that was a detail. The Ashburys had remained at Bosco till that establishment was favoured with the tidings that so nearly concerned it (they were communicated to Maud's mother by the housekeeper), and then the beautiful sufferer had found in her defeat strength to seek another asylum. The two ladies had departed for a destination unknown; he didn't think they had turned up in London. Guy Firminger averred that there were precious portable objects which he was sure he should miss on returning to his country home.

He came every day to Chester Street, and was evidently much less bored than Mary had prefigured by this regular tribute to verisimilitude. It was amusement enough to see the progress of their comedy and to invent new touches for some of its scenes. The girl herself was amused; it was an opportunity like another for cleverness such as hers and had much in common with private theatricals, especially with the rehearsals, the most amusing part. Moreover she was good-natured enough to be really pleased at the service it was impossible for her not to acknowledge that she had rendered. Each of the parties to this queer contract had anecdotes and suggestions for the other, and each reminded the other duly that they must at every step keep their story straight. Except for the exercise of this care Mary Gosselin found her duties less onerous than she had feared and her part in general much more passive than active. It consisted indeed largely of murmuring thanks and smiling and looking happy and handsome; as well as perhaps also in saying in answer to many questions that nothing as yet was fixed and of trying to remain humble when people expressed without ceremony that such a match was a wonder for such a girl. Her mother on the other hand was devotedly active. She treated the situation with private humour but with public zeal and, making it both real and ideal, told so many fibs about it that there were none left for Mary. The girl had failed to understand Mrs. Gosselin's interest in this elaborate pleasantry; the good lady had seen in it from the first more than she herself had been able to see. Mary performed her task mechanically, sceptically, but Mrs. Gosselin attacked hers with conviction and had really the air at moments of thinking that their fable had crystallised into fact. Mary allowed her as little of this attitude as possible and was ironical about her duplicity; warnings which the elder lady received with gaiety until one day when repetition had made them act on her nerves. Then she begged her daughter, with sudden asperity, not to talk to her as if she were a fool. She had already had words with Hugh about some aspects of the affair—so much as this was evident in Chester Street; a smothered discussion which at the moment had determined the poor boy to go to Paris with Bolton-Brown. The young men came back together after Mary had been "engaged" three weeks, but she remained in ignorance of what passed between Hugh and his mother the night of his return. She had gone to the opera with Lady Whiteroy, after one of her invariable comments on Mrs. Gosselin's invariable remark that of course Guy Firminger would spend his evening in their box. The remedy for his trouble, Lord Beaupré's prospective bride had said, was surely worse than the disease; she was in perfect good faith when she wondered that his lordship's sacrifices, his laborious cultivation of appearances should "pay."

Hugh Gosselin dined with his mother and at dinner talked of Paris and of what he had seen and done there; he kept the conversation superficial and after he had heard how his sister, at the moment, was occupied, asked no question that might have seemed to denote an interest in the success of the experiment for which in going abroad he had declined responsibility. His mother could not help observing that he never mentioned Guy Firminger by either of his names, and it struck her as a part of the same detachment that later, up stairs (she sat with him while he smoked), he should suddenly say as he finished a cigar:

"I return to New York next week."

"Before your time? What for?" Mrs. Gosselin was horrified.

"Oh, mamma, you know what for!"

"Because you still resent poor Mary's good-nature?"

"I don't understand it, and I don't like things I don't understand; therefore I'd rather not be here to see it. Besides I really can't tell a pack of lies."

Mrs. Gosselin exclaimed and protested; she had arguments to prove that there was no call at present for the least deflection from the truth; all that any one had to reply to any question (and there could be none that was embarrassing save the ostensible determination of the date of the marriage) was that nothing was settled as yet—a form of words in which for the life of her she couldn't see any perjury. "Why, then, go in for anything in such bad taste, to culminate only in something so absurd?" Hugh demanded. "If the essential part of the matter can't be spoken of as fixed nothing is fixed, the deception becomes transparent and they give the whole idea away. It's child's play."

"That's why it's so innocent. All I can tell you is that practically their attitude answers; he's delighted with its success. Those dreadful women have given him up; they've already found some other victim."

"And how is it all to end, please?"

Mrs. Gosselin was silent a moment. "Perhaps it won't end."

"Do you mean that the engagement will become real?"

Again the good lady said nothing until she broke out: "My dear boy, can't you trust your poor old mummy?"

"Is *that* your speculation? Is that Mary's? I never heard of anything so odious!" Hugh Gosselin cried. But she defended his sister with eagerness, with a gloss of coaxing, maternal indignation, declaring that Mary's disinterestedness was complete—she had the perfect proof of it. Hugh was conscious as he lighted another cigar that the conversation was more fundamental than any that he had ever had with his mother, who however hung fire but for an instant when he asked her what this "perfect proof" might be. He didn't doubt of his sister, he admitted that; but the perfect proof would make the whole thing more luminous. It took finally the form of a confession from Mrs. Gosselin that the girl evidently liked—well, greatly liked—Mr. Bolton-Brown. Yes, the good lady had seen for herself at Bosco that the smooth young American was making up to her and that, time and opportunity aiding, something might very well happen which could not be regarded as satisfactory. She had been very frank with Mary, had besought her not to commit herself to a suitor who in the very nature of the case couldn't meet the most legitimate of their views. Mary, who pretended not to know what their "views" were, had denied that she was in danger; but Mrs. Gosselin had assured her that she had all the air of it and had said triumphantly: "Agree to what Lord Beaupré asks of you, and I'll *believe* you." Mary had wished to be believed—so she had agreed. That was all the witchcraft any one had used.

Mrs. Gosselin out-talked her son, but there were two or three plain questions that he came back to; and the first of these bore upon the ground of her aversion to poor Bolton-Brown. He told her again, as he had told her before, that his friend was that rare bird a maker of money who was also a man of culture. He was a gentleman to his finger-tips, accomplished, capable, kind, with a charming mother and two lovely sisters (she should see them!) the sort of fellow in short whom it was stupid not to appreciate.

"I believe it all, and if I had three daughters he should be very welcome to one of them."

"You might easily have had three daughters who wouldn't attract him at all! You've had the good fortune to have one who does, and I think you do wrong to interfere with it."

"My eggs are in one basket then, and that's a reason the more for preferring Lord Beaupré," said Mrs. Gosselin.

"Then it *is* your calculation—?" stammered Hugh in dismay; on which she coloured and requested that he would be a little less rough with his mother. She would rather part with him immediately, sad as that would be, than that he should attempt to undo what she had done. When Hugh replied that it was not to Mary but to Beaupré himself that he judged it important he should speak, she informed him that a rash remonstrance might do his sister a cruel wrong. Dear Guy was *most* attentive.

"If you mean that he really cares for her there's the less excuse for his taking such a liberty with her. He's either in love with her or he isn't. If he is, let him make her a serious offer; if he isn't, let him leave her alone."

Mrs. Gosselin looked at her son with a kind of patient joy. "He's in love with her, but he doesn't know it."

"He ought to know it, and if he's so idiotic I don't see that we ought to consider him."

"Don't worry—he *shall* know it!" Mrs. Gosselin cried; and, continuing to struggle with Hugh, she insisted on the delicacy of the situation. She made a certain impression on him, though on confused grounds; she spoke at one moment as if he was to forbear because the matter was a make-believe that happened to contain a convenience for a distressed friend, and at another as if one ought to strain a point because there were great possibilities at stake. She was most lucid when she pictured the social position and other advantages of a peer of the realm. What had those of an American stockbroker, however amiable and with whatever shrill belongings in the background, to compare with them? She was inconsistent, but she was diplomatic, and the result of the discussion was that Hugh Gosselin became conscious of a dread of "injuring" his sister. He became conscious at the same time of a still greater apprehension, that of seeing her arrive at the agreeable in a tortuous, a second-rate manner. He might keep the peace to please his mother, but he couldn't enjoy it, and he actually took his departure, travelling in company with Bolton-Brown, who of course before going waited on the ladies in Chester Street to thank them for the kindness they had shown him. It couldn't be kept from Guy Firminger that Hugh was not happy, though when they met, which was only once or twice before he quitted London, Mary Gosselin's brother flattered himself that he was too proud to show it. He had always liked old loafing Guy and it was disagreeable to him not to like him now; but he was aware that he must either quarrel with him definitely or not at all and that he had passed his word to his mother. Therefore his attitude was strictly negative; he took with the parties to it no notice whatever of the "engagement," and he couldn't help it if to other people he had the air of not being initiated. They doubtless thought him strangely fastidious. Perhaps he was; the tone of London struck him in some respects as very horrid; he had grown in a manner away from it. Mary was impenetrable; tender, gay, charming, but with no patience, as she said, for his premature flight. Except when Lord Beaupré was present you would not have dreamed that he existed for her. In his company—he had to be present more or less of course—she was simply like any other English girl who disliked effusiveness. They had each the same manner, that of persons of rather a shy tradition who were on their guard against public "spooning." They practised their fraud with good taste, a good taste mystifying to Bolton-Brown, who thought their precautions excessive. When he took leave of Mary Gosselin her eyes consented for a moment to look deep down into his. He had been from the first of the opinion that they were beautiful, and he was more mystified than ever.

If Guy Firminger had failed to ask Hugh Gosselin whether he had a fault to find with what they were doing, this was, in spite of old friendship, simply because he was too happy now to care much whom he didn't please, to care at any rate for criticism. He had ceased to be critical himself, and his high prosperity could take his blamelessness for granted. His happiness would have been offensive if people generally hadn't liked him, for it consisted of a kind of monstrous candid comfort. To take all sorts of things for granted was still his great, his delightful characteristic; but it didn't prevent his showing imagination and tact and taste in particular circumstances. He made, in their little comedy, all the right jokes and none of the wrong ones: the girl had an acute sense that there were some jokes that would have been detestable. She gathered that it was universally supposed she was having an unprecedented season, and something of the glory of an enviable future seemed indeed to hang about her. People no doubt thought it odd that she didn't go about more with her future husband; but those who knew anything about her knew that she had never done exactly as other girls did. She had her own ways, her own freedoms and her own scruples. Certainly he made the London weeks much richer than they had ever been for a subordinate young person; he put more things into them, so that they grew dense and complicated. This frightened her at moments, especially when she thought with compunction that she was deceiving her very friends. She didn't mind taking the vulgar world in, but there were people she hated not to enlighten, to reassure. She could undeceive no one now, and indeed she would have been ashamed. There were hours when she wanted to stop— she had such a dread of doing too much; hours when she thought with dismay that the fiction of the rupture was still to come, with its horrid train of new untrue things. She spoke of it repeatedly to her confederate, who only postponed and postponed, told her she would never dream of forsaking him if she measured the good she was doing him. She did measure it however when she met him in the great world; she was of course always meeting him: that was the only way appearances were kept up. There was a certain attitude she could allow him to take on these occasions; it covered and carried off their subterfuge. He could talk to her unmolested; for herself she never spoke of anything but the charming girls, everywhere present, among whom he could freely choose. He didn't protest, because to choose freely was what he wanted, and they discussed these young ladies one by one. Some she recommended, some she disparaged, but it was almost the only subject she tolerated. It was her system in short, and she wondered he didn't get tired of it; she was so tired of it herself.

She tried other things that she thought he might find wearisome, but his good-humour was magnificent. He was now really for the first time enjoying his promotion, his wealth, his insight into the terms on which the world offered itself to the happy few, and these terms made a mixture healing to irritation. Once, at some glittering ball, he asked her if she should be jealous if he were to dance again with Lady Whiteroy, with whom he had danced already, and this was the only occasion on which he had come near making a joke of the wrong sort. She showed him what she thought of it and made him feel that the way to be forgiven was to spend the rest of the evening with that lovely creature. Now that the phalanx of the pressingly nubile was held in check there was accordingly nothing to prevent his passing his time pleasantly. Before he had taken this effective way the diplomatic mother, when she spied him flirting with a married woman, felt that in urging a virgin daughter's superior claims she worked for righteousness as well as for the poor girl. But Mary Gosselin protected these scandals practically by the still greater scandal of her indifference; so that he was in the odd position of having waited to be confined to know what it was to be at large. He had in other words the maximum of security with the minimum of privation. The lovely creatures of Lady Whiteroy's order thought Mary Gosselin charming, but they were the first to see through her falsity.

All this carried our precious pair to the middle of July; but nearly a month before that, one night under the summer stars, on the deck of the steamer that was to reach New York on the morrow, something had passed between Hugh Gosselin and his brooding American friend. The night was warm and splendid; these were their last hours at sea, and Hugh, who had been playing whist in the cabin, came up very late to take an observation before turning in. It was in this way that he chanced on his companion, who was leaning over the stern of the ship and gazing off, beyond its phosphorescent track, at the muffled, moaning ocean, the backward darkness, everything he had relinquished. Hugh stood by him for a moment and then asked him what he was thinking about. Bolton-Brown gave at first no answer; after which he turned round and, with his back against the guard of the deck, looked up at the multiplied stars. "He has it badly," Hugh Gosselin mentally commented. At last his friend replied: "About something you said yesterday."

"I forget what I said yesterday."

"You spoke of your sister's intended marriage; it was the only time you had spoken of it. You seemed to intimate that it might not after all take place."

Hugh hesitated a little. "Well, it *won't* take place. They're not engaged, not really. This is a secret, a preposterous secret. I wouldn't tell any one else, but I'm willing to tell you. It may make a difference to you."

Bolton-Brown turned his head; he looked at Hugh a minute through the fresh darkness. "It does make a difference to me. But I don't understand," he added.

"Neither do I. I don't like it. It's a pretence, a temporary make-believe, to help Beaupré through."

"Through what?"

"He's so run after."

The young American stared, ejaculated, mused. "Oh, yes—your mother told me."

"It's a sort of invention of my mother's and a notion of his own (very absurd, I think) till he can see his way. Mary serves as a kind of escort for these first exposed months. It's ridiculous, but I don't know that it hurts her."

"Oh!" said Bolton-Brown.

"I don't know either that it does her any good."

"No!" said Bolton-Brown. Then he added: "It's certainly very kind of her."

"It's a case of old friends," Hugh explained, inadequately as he felt. "He has always been in and out of our house."

"But how will it end?"

"I haven't the least idea."

Bolton-Brown was silent; he faced about to the stern again and stared at the rush of the ship. Then shifting his position once more: "Won't the engagement, before they've done, develop into the regular thing?"

Hugh felt as if his mother were listening. "I daresay not. If there were even a remote chance of that, Mary wouldn't have consented."

"But mayn't *he* easily find that—charming as she is—he's in love with her?"

"He's too much taken up with himself."

"That's just a reason," said Bolton-Brown. "Love is selfish." He considered a moment longer, then he went on: "And mayn't *she* find—?"

"Find what?" said Hugh, as he hesitated.

"Why, that she likes him."

"She likes him of course, else she wouldn't have come to his assistance. But her certainty about herself must have been just what made her not object to lending herself to the arrangement. She could do it decently because she doesn't seriously care for him. If she did—!" Hugh suddenly stopped.

"If she did?" his friend repeated.

"It would have been odious."

"I see," said Bolton-Brown gently. "But how will they break off?"

"It will be Mary who'll break off."

"Perhaps she'll find it difficult."

"She'll require a pretext."

"I see," mused Bolton-Brown, shifting his position again.

"She'll find one," Hugh declared.

"I hope so," his companion responded.

For some minutes neither of them spoke; then Hugh asked: "Are you in love with her?"

"Oh, my dear fellow!" Bolton-Brown wailed. He instantly added: "Will it be any use for me to go back?"

Again Hugh felt as if his mother were listening. But he answered: "*Do* go back."

"It's awfully strange," said Bolton-Brown. "I'll go back."

"You had better wait a couple of months, you know."

"Mayn't I lose her then?"

"No—they'll drop it all."

"I'll go back!" the American repeated, as if he hadn't heard. He was restless, agitated; he had evidently been much affected. He fidgeted away dimly, moved up the level length of the deck. Hugh Gosselin lingered longer at the stern; he fell into the attitude in which he had found the other, leaning over it and looking back at the great vague distance they had come. He thought of his mother.

VI

To remind her fond parent of the vanity of certain expectations which she more than suspected her of entertaining, Mary Gosselin, while she felt herself intensely watched (it had all brought about a horrid new situation at home) produced every day some fresh illustration of the fact that people were no longer imposed upon. Moreover these illustrations were not invented; the girl believed in them, and when once she had begun to note them she saw them multiply fast. Lady Whiteroy, for one, was distinctly suspicious; she had taken the liberty more than once of asking the future Lady Beaupré what in the world was the matter with her. Brilliant figure as she was and occupied with her own pleasures, which were of a very independent nature, she had nevertheless constituted herself Miss Gosselin's social sponsor: she took a particular interest in her marriage, an interest all the greater as it rested not only on a freely-professed regard for her, but on a keen sympathy with the other party to the transaction. Lady Whiteroy, who was very pretty and very clever and whom Mary secretly but profoundly mistrusted, delighted in them both in short; so much so that Mary judged herself happy to be in a false position, so certain should she have been to be jealous had she been in a true one. This charming woman threw out inquiries that made the girl not care to meet her eyes; and Mary ended by forming a theory of the sort of marriage for Lord Beaupré that Lady Whiteroy really would have appreciated. It would have been a marriage to a fool, a marriage to Maud Ashbury or to Charlotte Firminger. She would have her reasons for preferring that; and, as regarded the actual prospect, she had only discovered that Mary was even more astute than herself.

It will be understood how much our young lady was on the crest of the wave when I mention that in spite of this complicated consciousness she was one of the ornaments (Guy Firminger was of course another) of the party entertained by her zealous friend and Lord Whiteroy during the Goodwood week. She came back to town with the firm intention of putting an end to a comedy which had more than ever become odious to her; in consequence of which she had on this subject with her fellow-comedian a scene—the scene she had dreaded—half-pathetic, half-ridiculous. He appealed to her, wrestled with her, took his usual ground that she was saving his life without really lifting a finger. He denied that the public was not satisfied with their pretexts for postponement, their explanations of delay; what else was expected of a man who would wish to celebrate his nuptials on a suitable scale, but who had the misfortune to have had, one after another, three grievous bereavements? He promised not to molest her for the next three months, to go away till his "mourning" was over, to go abroad, to let her do as she liked. He wouldn't come near her, he wouldn't even write (no one would know it), if she would let him keep up the mere form of their fiction; and he would let her off the very first instant he definitely perceived that this expedient had ceased to be effective. She couldn't judge of that—she must let *him* judge; and it was a matter in which she could surely trust to his honour.

Mary Gosselin trusted to it, but she insisted on his going away. When he took such a tone as that she couldn't help being moved; he breathed with such frank, generous lips on the irritation she had stored up against him. Guy Firminger went to Homburg, and if his confederate consented not to clip the slender thread by which this particular engagement still hung, she made very short work with every other. A dozen invitations, for Cowes, for the country, for Scotland, shimmered there before her, made a pathway of flowers, but she sent barbarous excuses. When her mother, aghast, said to her "What then will you do?" she replied in a very conclusive manner "I'll go home!" Mrs. Gosselin was wise enough not to struggle; she saw that the thread was delicate, that it must dangle in quiet air. She therefore travelled back with her daughter to homely Hampshire, feeling that they were people of less importance than they had been for many a week. On the August afternoons they sat again on the little lawn on which Guy Firminger had found them the day he first became eloquent about the perils of the desirable young bachelor; and it was on this very spot that, toward the end of the month, and with some surprise, they beheld Mr. Bolton-Brown once more approach. He had come back from America; he had arrived but a few days before; he was staying, of all places in the world, at the inn in the village.

His explanation of this caprice was of all explanations the oddest: he had come three thousand miles for the love of water-colour. There was nothing more sketchable than the sketchability of Hampshire—wasn't it celebrated, classic? and he was so good as to include Mrs. Gosselin's charming premises, and even their charming occupants, in his view of the field. He fell to work with speed, with a sort of feverish eagerness; he seemed possessed indeed by the frenzy of the brush. He sketched everything on the place, and when he had represented an object once he went straight at it again. His advent was soothing to Mary Gosselin, in spite of his nervous activity; it must be admitted indeed that at the moment he arrived she had already felt herself in quieter waters. The August afternoons, the relinquishment of London, the simplified life, had rendered her a service which, if she had freely qualified it, she would have described as a restoration of her self-respect. If poor Guy found any profit in such conditions as these there was no great reason to repudiate him. She had so completely shaken off responsibility that she took scarcely more than a languid interest in the fact, communicated to her by Lady Whiteroy, that Charlotte Firminger had also, as the newspapers said, "proceeded" to Homburg. Lady Whiteroy knew, for Lady Whiteroy had "proceeded" as well; her physician had discovered in her constitution a pressing need for the comfort imbibed in dripping matutinal tumblers. She chronicled Charlotte's presence, and even to some extent her behaviour, among the haunters of the spring, but it was not till some time afterwards that Mary learned how Miss Firminger's pilgrimage had been made under her ladyship's protection. This was a further sign that, like Mrs. Gosselin, Lady Whiteroy had ceased to struggle; she had, in town, only shrugged her shoulders ambiguously on being informed that Lord Beaupré's intended was going down to her stupid home.

The fulness of Mrs. Gosselin's renunciation was apparent during the stay of the young American in the neighbourhood of that retreat. She occupied herself with her knitting, her garden and the cares of a punctilious hospitality, but she had no appearance of any other occupation. When people came to tea Bolton-Brown was always there, and she had the self-control to attempt to say nothing that could assuage their natural surprise. Mrs. Ashbury came one day with poor Maud, and the two elder ladies, as they had done more than once before, looked for some moments into each other's eyes. This time it was not a look of defiance, it was rather—or it would have been for an observer completely in the secret—a look of reciprocity, of fraternity, a look of arrangement. There was however no one completely in the secret save perhaps Mary, and Mary didn't heed. The arrangement at any rate was ineffectual; Mrs. Gosselin might mutely say, over the young American's eager, talkative shoulders, "Yes, you may have him if you can get him:" the most rudimentary experiments demonstrated that he was not to be got. Nothing passed on this subject between Mary and her mother, whom the girl none the less knew to be holding her breath and continuing to watch. She counted it more and more as one unpleasant result of her conspiracy with Guy Firminger that it almost poisoned a relation that had always been sweet. It was to show that she was independent of it that she did as she liked now, which was almost always as Bolton-Brown liked. When in the first days of September—it was in the warm, clear twilight, and they happened, amid the scent of fresh hay, to be leaning side by side on a stile—he gave her a view of the fundamental and esoteric, as distinguished from the convenient and superficial motive of his having come back to England, she of course made no allusion to a prior tie. On the other hand she insisted on his going up to London by the first train the next day. He was to wait—that was distinctly understood—for his satisfaction.

She desired meanwhile to write immediately to Guy Firminger, but as he had kept his promise of not complicating their contract with letters she was uncertain as to his actual whereabouts: she was only sure he would have left Homburg. Lady Whiteroy had become silent, so there were no more sidelights, and she was on the point of telegraphing to London for an address when she received a telegram from Bosco. The proprietor of that seat had arrived there the day before, and he found he could make trains fit if she would on the morrow allow him to come over and see her for a day or two. He had returned sooner than their agreement allowed, but she answered "Come" and she showed his missive to her mother, who at the sight of it wept with strange passion. Mary said to her "For heaven's sake, don't let him see you!" She lost no time; she told him on the morrow as soon as he entered the house that she couldn't keep it up another hour.

"All right—it *is* no use," he conceded; "they're at it again!"

"You see you've gained nothing!" she replied triumphantly. She had instantly recognised that he was different, how much had happened.

"I've gained some of the happiest days of my life."

"Oh, that was not what you tried for!"

"Indeed it was, and I got exactly what I wanted," said Guy Firminger. They were in the cool little drawing-room where the morning light was dim. Guy Firminger had a sunburnt appearance, as in England people returning from other countries are apt to have, and Mary thought he had never looked so well. It was odd, but it was noticeable, that he had grown much handsomer since he had become a personage. He paused a moment, smiling at her while her mysterious eyes rested on him, and then he added: "Nothing ever worked better. It's no use now—people see. But I've got a start. I wanted to turn round and look about, and I *have* turned round and looked about. There are things I've escaped. I'm afraid you'll never understand how deeply I'm indebted to you."

"Oh, it's all right!" said Mary Gosselin.

There was another short silence, after which he went on: "I've come back sooner than I promised, but only to be strictly fair. I began to see that we couldn't hold out and that it was my duty to let you off. From that moment I was bound to put an end to your situation. I might have done so by letter, but that seemed scarcely decent. It's all I came back for, you know, and it's why I wired to you yesterday."

Mary hesitated an instant, she reflected intensely. What had happened, what would happen, was that if she didn't take care the signal for the end of their little arrangement would not have appeared to come from herself. She particularly wished it not to come from anyone else, she had even a horror of that; so that after an instant she hastened to say: "I was on the very point of wiring to *you*—I was only waiting for your address."

"Wiring to me?" He seemed rather blank.

"To tell you that our absurd affair really, this time, can't go on another day—to put a complete stop to it."

"Oh!" said Guy Firminger.

"So it's all right."

"You've always hated it!" Guy laughed; and his laugh sounded slightly foolish to the girl.

"I found yesterday that I hated it more than ever."

Lord Beaupré showed a quickened attention. "For what reason—yesterday?"

"I would rather not tell you, please. Perhaps some time you'll find it out."

He continued to look at her brightly and fixedly with his confused cheerfulness. Then he said with a vague, courteous alacrity: "I see, I see!" She had an impression that he didn't see; but it didn't matter, she was nervous and quite preferred that he shouldn't. They both got up, and in a moment he exclaimed: "Well, I'm intensely sorry it's over! It has been so charming."

"You've been very good about it; I mean very reasonable," Mary said, to say something. Then she felt in her nervousness that this was just what she ought not to have said: it sounded ironical and provoking, whereas she had meant it as pure good-nature. "Of course you'll stay to luncheon?" she continued. She was bound in common hospitality to speak of that, and he answered that it would give him the greatest pleasure. After this her apprehension increased, and it was confirmed in particular by the manner in which he suddenly asked:

"By the way, what reason shall we give?"

"What reason?"

"For our rupture. Don't let us seem to have quarrelled."

"We can't help that," said Mary. "Nothing else will account for our behaviour."

"Well, I sha'n't say anything about *you*."

"Do you mean you'll let people think it was yourself who were tired of it?"

"I mean I sha'n't *blame* you."

"You ought to behave as if you cared!" said Mary.

Guy Firminger laughed, but he looked worried and he evidently was puzzled. "You must act as if you had jilted me."

"You're not the sort of person unfortunately that people jilt."

Lord Beaupré appeared to accept this statement as incontestable; not with elation however, but with candid regret, the slightly embarrassed recognition of a fundamental obstacle. "Well, it's no one's business, at any rate, is it?"

"No one's, and that's what I shall say if people question me. Besides," Mary added, "they'll see for themselves."

"What will they see?"

"I mean they'll understand. And now we had better join mamma."

It was his evident inclination to linger in the room after he had said this that gave her complete alarm. Mrs. Gosselin was in another room, in which she sat in the morning, and Mary moved in that direction, pausing only in the hall for him to accompany her. She wished to get him into the presence of a third person. In the hall he joined her, and in doing so laid his hand gently on her arm. Then looking into her eyes with all the pleasantness of his honesty, he said: "It will be very easy for me to appear to care—for I *shall* care. I shall care immensely!" Lord Beaupré added smiling.

Anything, it struck her, was better than that—than that he should say: "We'll keep on, if you like (*I* should!) only this time it will be serious. Hold me to it—do; don't let me go; lead me on to the altar—really!" Some such words as these, she believed, were rising to his lips, and she had an insurmountable horror of hearing them. It was as if, well enough meant on *his* part, they would do her a sort of dishonour, so that all her impulse was quickly to avert them. That was not the way she wanted to be asked in marriage. "Thank you very much," she said, "but it doesn't in the least matter. You will seem to have been jilted—so it's all right!"

"All right! You mean—?" He hesitated, he had coloured a little: his eyes questioned her.

"I'm engaged to be married—in earnest."

"Oh!" said Lord Beaupré.

"You asked me just now if I had a special reason for having been on the point of telegraphing to you, and I said I had. That was my special reason."

"I see!" said Lord Beaupré. He looked grave for a few seconds, then he gave an awkward smile. But he behaved with perfect tact and discretion, didn't even ask her who the gentleman in the case might be. He congratulated her in the dark, as it were, and if the effect of this was indeed a little odd she liked him for his quick perception of the fine fitness of pulling up short. Besides, he extracted the name of the gentleman soon enough from her mother, in whose company they now immediately found themselves. Mary left Guy Firminger with the good lady for half an hour before luncheon; and when the girl came back it was to observe that she had been crying again. It was dreadful—what she might have been saying. Their guest, however, at luncheon was not lachrymose; he was natural, but he was talkative and gay. Mary liked the way he now behaved, and more particularly the way he departed immediately after the meal. As soon as he was gone Mrs. Gosselin broke out suppliantly: "Mary!" But her daughter replied:

"I know, mamma, perfectly what you're going to say, and if you attempt to say it I shall leave the room." With this threat (day after day, for the following time) she kept the terrible appeal unuttered until it was too late for an appeal to be of use. That afternoon she wrote to Bolton-Brown that she accepted his offer of marriage.

Guy Firminger departed altogether; he went abroad again and to far countries. He was therefore not able to be present at the nuptials of Miss Gosselin and the young American whom he had entertained at Bosco, which took place in the middle of November. Had he been in England however he probably would have felt impelled by a due regard for past verisimilitude to abstain from giving his countenance to such an occasion. His absence from the country contributed to the needed even if astonishing effect of his having been jilted; so, likewise, did the reputed vastness of Bolton-Brown's young income, which in London was grossly exaggerated. Hugh Gosselin had perhaps a little to do with this; as he had sacrificed a part of his summer holiday, he got another month and came out to his sister's wedding. He took public comfort in his brother-in-law; nevertheless he listened with attention to a curious communication made him by his mother after the young couple had started for Italy; even to the point of bringing out the inquiry (in answer to her assertion that poor Guy had been ready to place everything he had at Mary's feet): "Then why the devil didn't he do it?"

"From simple delicacy! He didn't want to make her feel as if she had lent herself to an artifice only on purpose to get hold of him—to treat her as if she too had been at bottom one of the very harpies she helped him to elude."

Hugh thought a moment. "That *was* delicate."

"He's the dearest creature in the world. He's on his guard, he's prudent, he tested himself by separation. Then he came back to England in love with her. She might have had it all!"

"I'm glad she didn't get it *that* way."

"She had only to wait—to put an end to their artifice, harmless as it was, for the present, but still wait. She might have broken off in a way that would have made it come on again better."

"That's exactly what she didn't want."

"I mean as a quite separate incident," said Mrs. Gosselin.

"*I* loathed their artifice, harmless as it was!" her son observed.

Mrs. Gosselin for a moment made no answer; then she turned away from the fire into which she had been pensively gazing with the ejaculation "Poor dear Guy!"

"I can't for the life of me see that he's to be pitied."

"He'll marry Charlotte Firminger."

"If he's such an ass as that it's his own affair."

"Bessie Whiteroy will bring it about."

"What has *she* to do with it?"

"She wants to get hold of him."

"Then why will she marry him to another woman?"

"Because in that way she can select the other—a woman he won't care for. It will keep him from taking some one that's nicer."

Hugh Gosselin stared—he laughed aloud. "Lord, mamma, you're deep!"

"Indeed I am, I see much more."

"What do you see?"

"Mary won't in the least care for America. Don't tell me she will," Mrs. Gosselin added, "for you know perfectly you don't believe it."

"She'll care for her husband, she'll care for everything that concerns him."

"He's very nice, in his little way he's delightful. But as an alternative to Lord Beaupré he's ridiculous!"

"Mary's in a position in which she has nothing to do with alternatives."

"For the present, yes, but not for ever. She'll have enough of your New York; they'll come back here. I see the future dark," Mrs. Gosselin pursued, inexorably musing.

"Tell me then all you see."

"She'll find poor Guy wretchedly married, and she'll be very sorry for him."

"Do you mean that he'll make love to her? You give a queer account of your paragon."

"He'll value her sympathy. I see life as it is."

"You give a queer account of your daughter."

"I don't give *any* account. She'll behave perfectly," Mrs. Gosselin somewhat inconsequently subjoined.

"Then what are you afraid of?"

"She'll be sorry for him, and it will be all a worry."

"A worry to whom?"

The good lady was silent a moment. "To me," she replied. "And to you as well."

"Then they mustn't come back."

"That will be a greater worry still."

"Surely not a greater—a smaller. We'll put up with the lesser evil."

"Nothing will prevent her coming to a sense, eventually, of what *might* have been. And when they *both* recognize it——"

"It will be very dreadful!" Hugh exclaimed, completing gaily his mother's phrase. "I don't see, however," he added, "what in all this you do with Bessie Whiteroy."

"Oh, he'll be tired of her; she's hard, she'll have become despotic. I see life as it is," the good lady repeated.

"Then all I can say is that it's not very nice! But they sha'n't come back: *I'll* attend to that!" said Hugh Gosselin, who has attended to it up to this time successfully, though the rest of his mother's prophecy is so far accomplished (it was her second hit) as that Charlotte Firminger is now, strange as it may seem, Lady Beaupré.

THE VISITS

The other day, after her death, when they were discussing her, someone said in reference to the great number of years she had lived, the people she had seen and the stories she knew: "What a pity no one ever took any notes of her talk!" For a London epitaph that was almost exhaustive, and the subject presently changed. One of the listeners had taken many notes, but he didn't confess it on the spot. The following story is a specimen of my exactitude—I took it down, *verbatim*, having that faculty, the day after I heard it. I choose it, at hazard, among those of her reminiscences that I have preserved; it's not worse than the others. I will give you some of the others too—when occasion offers—so that you may judge.

I met in town that year a dear woman whom I had scarcely seen since I was a girl; she had dropped out of the world; she came up but once in five years. We had been together as very young creatures, and then we had married and gone our ways. It was arranged between us that after I should have paid a certain visit in August in the west of England I would take her—it would be very convenient, she was just over the Cornish border—on the way to my other engagements: I would work her in, as you say nowadays. She wanted immensely to show me her home, and she wanted still more to show me her girl, who had not come up to London, choosing instead, after much deliberation, to go abroad for a month with her brother and her brother's coach—he had been cramming for something—and Mrs. Coach of course. All that Mrs. Chantry had been able to show me in town was her husband, one of those country gentlemen with a moderate property and an old place who are a part of the essence in their own neighbourhood and not a part of anything anywhere else.

A couple of days before my visit to Chantry Court the people to whom I had gone from town took me over to see some friends of theirs who lived, ten miles away, in a place that was supposed to be fine. As it was a long drive we stayed to luncheon; and then as there were gardens and other things that were more or less on show we struggled along to tea, so as to get home just in time for dinner. There were a good many other people present, and before luncheon a very pretty girl came into the drawing-room, a real maiden in her flower, less than twenty, fresh and fair and charming, with the expression of some one I knew. I asked who she was, and was told she was Miss Chantry, so that in a moment I spoke to her, mentioning that I was an old friend of her mother's and that I was coming to pay them a visit. She looked rather frightened and blank, was apparently unable to say that she had ever heard of me, and hinted at no pleasure in the idea that she was to hear of me again. But this didn't prevent my perceiving that she was lovely, for I was wise enough even then not to think it necessary to measure people by the impression that one makes on them. I saw that any I should make on Louisa Chantry would be much too clumsy a test. She had been staying at the house at which I was calling; she had come alone, as the people were old friends and to a certain extent neighbours, and was going home in a few days. It was a daughterless house, but there was inevitable young life: a couple of girls from the vicarage, a married son and his wife, a young man who had "ridden over" and another young man who was staying.

Louisa Chantry sat opposite to me at luncheon, but too far for conversation, and before we got up I had discovered that if her manner to me had been odd it was not because she was inanimate. She was on the contrary in a state of intense though carefully muffled vibration. There was some fever in her blood, but no one perceived it, no one, that is, with an exception—an exception which was just a part of the very circumstance. This single suspicion was lodged in the breast of the young man whom I have alluded to as staying in the house. He was on the same side of the table as myself and diagonally facing the girl; therefore what I learned about him was for the moment mainly what she told me; meaning by "she" her face, her eyes, her movements, her whole perverted personality. She was extremely on her guard, and I should never have guessed her secret but for an accident. The accident was that the only time she dropped her eyes upon him during the repast I happened to notice it. It might not have been much to notice, but it led to my seeing that there was a little drama going on and that the young man would naturally be the hero. It was equally natural that in this capacity he should be the cause of my asking my left-hand neighbour, who happened to be my host, for some account of him. But "Oh, that fellow? he's my nephew," was a description which, to appear copious, required that I should know more about the uncle.

We had coffee on the terrace of the house; a terrace laid out in one quarter, oddly and charmingly, in grass where the servants who waited upon us seemed to tread, processionally, on soundless velvet. There I had a good look at my host's nephew and a longer talk with my friend's daughter, in regard to whom I had become conscious of a faint, formless anxiety. I remember saying to her, gropingly, instinctively: "My dear child, can I do anything for you? I shall perhaps see your mother before you do. Can I for instance say anything to her *from* you?" This only made her blush and turn away; and it was not till too many days had passed that I guessed that what had looked out at me unwittingly in her little gazing trepidation was something like "Oh, just take me away in spite of myself!" Superficially, conspicuously, there was nothing in the young man to take her away from.

He was a person of the middle condition, and save that he didn't look at all humble might have passed for a poor relation. I mean that he had rather a seedy, shabby air, as if he were wearing out old clothes (he had on faded things that didn't match); and I formed vaguely the theory that he was a specimen of the numerous youthful class that goes to seek its fortune in the colonies, keeps strange company there and comes home without a penny. He had a brown, smooth, handsome face, a slightly swaggering, self-conscious ease, and was probably objected to in the house. He hung about, smoking cigarettes on the terrace, and nobody seemed to have much to say to him—a circumstance which, as he managed somehow to convey, left him absolutely indifferent. Louisa Chantry strolled away with one of the girls from the vicarage; the party on the terrace broke up and the nephew disappeared.

It was settled that my friends and I should take leave at half-past five, and I begged to be abandoned in the interval to my devices. I turned into the library and, mounted on ladders, I handled old books and old prints and soiled my gloves. Most of the others had gone to look at the church, and I was left in possession. I wandered into the rooms in which I knew there were pictures; and if the pictures were not good there was some interesting china which I followed from corner to corner and from cabinet to cabinet. At last I found myself on the threshold of a small room which appeared to terminate the series and in which, between the curtains draping the doorways, there appeared to be rows of rare old plates on velvet screens. I was on the point of going in when I became aware that there was something else beside, something which threw me back. Two persons were standing side by side at the window, looking out together with their backs to me—two persons as to whom I immediately felt that they believed themselves to be alone and unwatched. One of them was Louisa Chantry, the other was the young man whom my host had described as his nephew. They were so placed as not to see me, and when I recognized them I checked myself instinctively. I hesitated a moment; then I turned away altogether. I can't tell you why, except that if I had gone in I should have had somehow the air of discovering them. There was no visible reason why they should have been embarrassed by discovery, inasmuch as, so far as I could see, they were doing no harm, were only standing more or less together, without touching, and for the moment apparently saying nothing. Were they watching something out of the window? I don't know; all I know is that the observation I had made at luncheon gave me a sense of responsibility. I might have taken my responsibility the other way and broken up their communion; but I didn't feel this to be sufficiently my business. Later on I wished I had.

I passed through the rooms again, and then out of the house. The gardens were ingenious, but they made me think (I have always that conceited habit) how much cleverer *I* should have been about them. Presently I met several of the rest of the party coming back from the church; on which my hostess took possession of me, declaring there was a point of view I must absolutely be treated to. I saw she was a walking woman and that this meant half a mile in the park. But I was good for that, and we wandered off together while the others returned to the house. It was present to me that I ought to ask my companion, for Helen Chantry's sake, a question about Louisa—whether for instance she had happened to notice the way the girl seemed to be going. But it was difficult to say anything without saying too much; so that to begin with I merely risked the observation that our young friend was remarkably pretty. As the point admitted of no discussion this didn't take us very far; nor was the subject much enlarged by our unanimity as to the fact that she was also remarkably nice. I observed that I had had very little chance to talk with her, for which I was sorry, having known her mother for years. My hostess, at this, looked vaguely round, as if she had missed her for the first time. "Sure enough, she has not been about. I daresay she's been writing to her mother—she's always writing to her mother." "Not always," I mentally reflected; but I waited discreetly, admiring everything and rising to the occasion and the views, before I inquired casually who the young man might be who had sat two or three below me at luncheon—the rather good-looking young man, with the regular features and the brownish clothes—not the one with the moustache.

"Oh, poor Jack Brandon," said my companion, in a tone calculated to make him seem no one in particular.

"Is he very poor?" I asked, with a laugh.

"Oh dear, yes. There are nine of them—fancy!—all boys; and there's nothing for anyone but the eldest. He's my husband's nephew—his poor mother's my sister-in-law. He sometimes turns up here when he has nothing better to do; but I don't think he likes us much." I saw she meant that they didn't like *him*; and I exposed myself to suspicion by asking if he had been with them long. But my friend was not very plastic, and she simplified my whole theory of the case by replying after she had thought a moment that she wasn't clear about it—she thought he had come only the morning before. It seemed to me I could safely feel a little further, so I inquired if he were likely to stay many days. "Oh dear, no; he'll go tomorrow!" said my hostess. There was nothing whatever to show that she saw a connection between my odd interest in Mr. Brandon and the subject of our former reference; there was only a quick lucidity on the subject of the young man's departure. It reassured me, for no great complications would have arisen in forty-eight hours.

In retracing our steps we passed again through a part of the gardens. Just after we had entered them my hostess, begging me to excuse her, called at a man who was raking leaves to ask him a question about his wife. I heard him reply "Oh, she's very bad, my lady," and I followed my course. Presently my lady turned round with him, as if to go to see his wife, who apparently was ill and on the place. I continued to look about me—there were such charming things; and at the end of five minutes I missed my way—I had not taken the direction of the house. Suddenly at the turn of a walk, the angle of a great clipped hedge, I found myself face to face with Jack Brandon. He was moving rapidly, looking down, with his hands in his pockets, and he started and stared at me a moment. I said "Oh, how d'ye do?" and I was on the point of adding "Won't you kindly show me the right way?" But with a summary salute and a queer expression of face he had already passed me. I looked after him an instant and I all but stopped him; then one of the faintest voices of the air told me that Louisa Chantry would not be far off, that in fact if I were to go on a few steps I should find her. I continued and I passed through an arched aperture of the hedge, a kind of door in the partition. This corner of the place was like an old French garden, a little inclosed apartment, with statues set into the niches of the high walls of verdure. I paused in admiration; then just opposite to me I saw poor Louisa. She was on a bench, with her hands clasped in her lap, her head bent, her eyes staring down before her. I advanced on the grass, attracting her attention; and I was close to her before she looked at me, before she sprang up and showed me a face convulsed with nameless pain. She was so pale that I thought she was ill—I had a vision of her companion's having rushed off for help. She stood gazing at me with expanded eyes and parted lips, and what I was mainly conscious of was that she had become ten years older. Whatever troubled her it was something pitiful—something that prompted me to hold out my two hands to her and exclaim tenderly "My poor child, my poor child!" She wavered a moment, as if she wanted to escape me but couldn't trust herself to run; she looked away from me, turning her head this way and that. Then as I went close to her she covered her face with her two hands, she let me lay mine upon her and draw her to my breast. As she dropped her head upon it she burst into tears, sobbing soundlessly and tragically. I asked her no question, I only held her so long as she would, letting her pour out the passion which I felt at the same time she made a tremendous effort to smother. She couldn't smother it, but she could break away violently; and this she quickly did, hurrying out of the nook where our little scene—and some other greater scene, I judged, just before it—had taken place, and leaving me infinitely mystified. I sat down on the bench a moment and thought it over; then I succeeded in discovering a path to the house.

The carriage was at the door for our drive home, but my companions, who had had tea, were waiting for our hostess, of whom they wished to take leave and who had not yet come in. I reported her as engaged with the wife of one of the gardeners, but we lingered a little in the hall, a largeish group, to give her time to arrive. Two other persons were absent, one of whom was Louisa Chantry and the other the young man whom I had just seen quitting her in the garden. While I sat there, a trifle abstracted, still somewhat agitated by the sequel to that incident and at the same time impatient of our last vague dawdle, one of the footmen presented me with a little folded note. I turned away to open it, and at the very moment our hostess fortunately came in. This diverted the attention of the others from the action of the footman, whom, after I had looked at the note, I immediately followed into the drawing-room. He led me through it and through two or three others to the door of the little retreat in which, nearly an hour before, I had come upon Louisa Chantry and Mr. Brandon. The note was from Louisa, it contained the simple words "Would you very kindly speak to me an instant before you go?" She was waiting for me in the most sequestered spot she had been able to select, and there the footman left us. The girl came straight at me and in an instant she had grasped my hands. I became aware that her condition had changed; her tears were gone, she had a concentrated purpose. I could scarcely see her beautiful young face—it was pressed, beseechingly, so close to mine. I only felt, as her dry, shining eyes almost dazzled me, that a strong light had been waved back and forth before me. Her words at first seemed to me incoherent; then I understood that she was asking me for a pledge.

"Excuse me, forgive me for bringing you here—to say something I can't say before all those people. *Do* forgive me—it was so awfully kind of you to come. I couldn't think of any other way—just for two seconds. I want you to swear to me," she went on, with her hands now raised and intensely clasped.

"To swear, dearest child?"

"I'm not your dearest child—I'm not anyone's! But *don't* tell mamma. Promise me—promise me," she insisted.

"Tell her what?—I don't understand."

"Oh, you do—you do!" she kept on; "and if you're going to Chantry you'll see her, you'll be with her, you may see her before I do. On my knees I ask you for a vow!"

She seemed on the point of throwing herself at my feet, but I stopped her, I kept her erect. "When shall *you* see your mother?"

"As soon as I can. I want to get home—I want to get home!" With this I thought she was going to cry again, but she controlled herself and only pressed me with feverish eyes.

"You have some great trouble—for heaven's sake tell me what it is."

"It isn't anything—it will pass. Only don't breathe it to mamma!"

"How can I breathe it if I don't know what it is?"

"You do know—you know what I mean." Then after an instant's pause she added: "What I did in the garden."

"*What* did you do in the garden?"

"I threw myself on your neck and I sobbed—I behaved like a maniac."

"Is that all you mean?"

"It's what I don't want mamma to know—it's what I beseech you to keep silent about. If you don't I'll never, never go home. Have *mercy* on me!" the poor child quavered.

"Dear girl, I only want to be tender to you—to be perfect. But tell me first: has anyone acted wrongly to you?"

"No one—*no* one. I speak the truth."

She looked into my eyes, and I looked far into hers. They were wild with pain and yet they were so pure that they made me confusedly believe her. I hesitated a moment; then I risked the question: "Isn't Mr. Brandon responsible for anything?"

"For nothing—for nothing! Don't blame *him*!" the girl passionately cried.

"He hasn't made love to you?"

"Not a word—before God! Oh, it was too awful!" And with this she broke away from me, flung herself on her knees before a sofa, burying her face in it and in her arms. "Promise me, promise me, promise me!" she continued to wail.

I was horribly puzzled but I was immeasurably touched. I stood looking a moment at her extravagant prostration; then I said "I'm dreadfully in the dark, but I promise."

This brought her to her feet again, and again she seized my hands. "Solemnly, sacredly?" she panted.

"Solemnly, sacredly."

"Not a syllable—not a hint?"

"Dear Louisa," I said kindly, "when I promise I perform."

"You see I don't know you. And when do you go to Chantry?"

"Day after to-morrow. And when do you?"

"To-morrow if I can."

"Then you'll see your mother first—it will be all right," I said smiling.

"All right, all right!" she repeated, with her woeful eyes. "Go, go!" she added, hearing a step in the adjoining room.

The footman had come back to announce that my friends were seated in the carriage, and I was careful to say before him in a different tone: "Then there's nothing more I can do for you?"

"Nothing—good-bye," said Louisa, tearing herself away too abruptly to take my kiss, which, to follow the servant again, I left unbestowed. I felt awkward and guilty as I took leave of the company, murmuring something to my entertainers about having had an arrangement to make with Miss Chantry. Most of the people bade us good-bye from the steps, but I didn't see Jack Brandon. On our drive home in the waning afternoon my other friends doubtless found me silent and stupid.

I went to Chantry two days later, and was disappointed to find that the daughter of the house had not returned, though indeed after parting with her I had been definitely of the opinion that she was much more likely to go to bed and be ill. Her mother however had not heard that she was ill, and my inquiry about the young lady was of course full of circumspection. It was a little difficult, for I had to talk about her, Helen being particularly delighted that we had already made acquaintance. No day had been fixed for her return, but it came over my friend that she oughtn't to be absent during too much of my visit. She was the best thing they had to show—she was the flower and the charm of the place. It had other charms as well—it was a sleepy, silvery old home, exquisitely grey and exquisitely green; a house where you could have confidence in your leisure: it would be as genuine as the butter and the claret. The very look of the pleasant, prosaic drawing-room suggested long mornings of fancy work, of Berlin wool and premeditated patterns, new stitches and mild pauses. My good Helen was always in the middle of something eternal, of which the past and the future were rolled up in oilcloth and tissue paper, and the intensest moments of conversation were when it was spread out for pensive opinions. These used to drop sometimes even from Christopher Chantry when he straddled vaguely in with muddy leggings and the raw materials of a joke. He had a mind like a large, full milk-pan, and his wit was as thick as cream.

One evening I came down to dinner a little early and, to my surprise, found my troubled maiden in possession of the drawing-room. She was evidently troubled still, and had been waiting there in the hope of seeing me alone. We were too quickly interrupted by her parents, however, and I had no conversation with her till I sat down to the piano after dinner and beckoned to her to come and stand by it. Her father had gone off to smoke; her mother dozed by one of the crackling little fires of the summer's end.

"Why didn't you come home the day you told me you meant to?"

She fixed her eyes on my hands. "I couldn't, I couldn't!"

"You look to me as if you were very ill."

"I am," the girl said simply.

"You ought to see some one. Something ought to be done."

She shook her head with quiet despair. "It would be no use—no one would know."

"What do you mean—would know?"

"No one would understand."

"You ought to make them!"

"Never—never!" she repeated. "Never!"

"I confess *I* don't," I replied, with a kind of angry renunciation. I played louder, with the passion of my uneasiness and the aggravation of my responsibility.

"No, you don't indeed," said Louisa Chantry.

I had only to accept this disadvantage, and after a moment I went on: "What became of Mr. Brandon?"

"I don't know."

"Did he go away?"

"That same evening."

"Which same evening?"

"The day you were there. I never saw him again."

I was silent a minute, then I risked: "And you never will, eh?"

"Never—never."

"Then why shouldn't you get better?"

She also hesitated, after which she answered: "Because I'm going to die."

My music ceased, in spite of me, and we sat looking at each other. Helen Chantry woke up with a little start and asked what was the matter. I rose from the piano and I couldn't help saying "Dear Helen, I haven't the least idea." Louisa sprang up, pressing her hand to her left side, and the next instant I cried aloud "She's faint—she's ill—do come to her!" Mrs. Chantry bustled over to us, and immediately afterwards the girl had thrown herself on her mother's breast, as she had thrown herself days before on mine; only this time without tears, without cries, in the strangest, most tragic silence. She was not faint, she was only in despair—that at least is the way I really saw her. There was something in her contact that scared poor Helen, that operated a sudden revelation: I can see at this hour the queer frightened look she gave me over Louisa's shoulder. The girl however in a moment disengaged herself, declaring that she was not ill, only tired, very tired, and wanted to go to bed. "Take her, take her—go with her," I said to her mother; and I pushed them, got them out of the room, partly to conceal my own trepidation. A few moments after they had gone Christopher Chantry came in, having finished his cigar, and I had to mention to him—to explain their absence—that his daughter was so fatigued that she had withdrawn under her mother's superintendence. "Didn't she seem done up, awfully done up? What on earth, at that confounded place, did she go in for?" the dear man asked with his pointless kindness. I couldn't tell him this was just what I myself wanted to know; and while I pretended to read I wondered inextinguishably what indeed she had "gone in" for. It had become still more difficult to keep my vow than I had expected; it was also very difficult that evening to converse with Christopher Chantry. His wife's continued absence rendered some conversation necessary; yet it had the advantage of making him remark, after it had lasted an hour, that he must go to see what was the matter. He left me, and soon afterwards I betook myself to my room; bedtime was elastic in the early sense at Chantry. I knew I should only have to wait awhile for Helen to come to me, and in fact by eleven o'clock she arrived.

"She's in a very strange state—something happened there."

"And *what* happened, pray?"

"I can't make out; she won't tell me."

"Then what makes you suppose so?"

"She has broken down utterly; she says there was something."

"Then she does tell you?"

"Not a bit. She only begins and then stops short—she says it's too dreadful."

"Too dreadful?"

"She says it's *horrible*," my poor friend murmured, with tears in her eyes and tragic speculation in her mild maternal face.

"But in what way? Does she give you no facts, no clue?"

"It was something she did."

We looked at each other a moment. "Did?" I echoed. "Did to whom?"

"She won't tell me—she says she *can't*. She tries to bring it out, but it sticks in her throat."

"Nonsense. She did nothing," I said.

"What *could* she do?" Helen asked, gazing at me.

"She's ill, she's in a fever, her mind's wandering."

"So I say to her father."

"And what does *she* say to him?"

"Nothing—she won't speak to him. He's with her now, but she only lies there letting him hold her hand, with her face turned away from him and her eyes closed."

"You must send for the doctor immediately."

"I've already sent for him."

"Should you like me to sit up with her?"

"Oh, I'll do that!" Helen said. Then she asked: "But if you were there the other day, what did you see?"

"Nothing whatever," I resolutely answered.

"*Really* nothing?"

"Really, my dear child."

"But was there nobody there who could have made up to her?"

I hesitated a moment. "My poor Helen, you should have seen them!"

"She wouldn't look at anybody that wasn't remarkably nice," Helen mused.

"Well—I don't want to abuse your friends—but nobody was remarkably nice. Believe me, she hasn't looked at anybody, and nothing whatever has occurred. She's ill, and it's a mere morbid fancy."

"It's a mere morbid fancy———!" Mrs. Chantry gobbled down this formula. I felt that I was giving her another still more acceptable, and which she as promptly adopted, when I added that Louisa would soon get over it.

I may as well say at once that Louisa never got over it. There followed an extraordinary week, which I look back upon as one of the most uncomfortable of my life. The doctor had something to say about the action of his patient's heart—it was weak and slightly irregular, and he was anxious to learn whether she had lately been exposed to any violent shock or emotion—but he could give no name to the disorder under the influence of which she had begun unmistakably to sink. She lay on the sofa in her room—she refused to go to bed, and in the absence of complications it was not insisted on—utterly white, weak and abstracted, shaking her head at all suggestion, waving away all nourishment save the infinitesimally little that enabled her to stretch out her hand from time to time (at intervals of very unequal length) and begin "Mother, mother!" as if she were mustering courage for a supreme confession. The courage never came; she was haunted by a strange impulse to speak, which in turn was checked on her lips by some deeper horror or some stranger fear. She seemed to seek relief spasmodically from some unforgettable consciousness and then to find the greatest relief of all in impenetrable silence. I knew these things only from her mother, for before me (I went gently in and out of her room two or three times a day) she gave no sign whatever. The little local doctor, after the first day, acknowledged himself at sea and expressed a desire to consult with a colleague at Exeter. The colleague journeyed down to us and shuffled and stammered: he recommended an appeal to a high authority in London. The high authority was summoned by telegraph and paid us a flying visit. He enunciated the valuable opinion that it was a very curious case and dropped the striking remark that in so charming a home a young lady ought to bloom like a flower. The young lady's late hostess came over, but she could throw no light on anything: all that she had ever noticed was that Louisa had seemed "rather blue" for a day or two before she brought her visit to a close. Our days were dismal enough and our nights were dreadful, for I took turns with Helen in sitting up with the girl. Chantry Court itself seemed conscious of the riddle that made its chambers ache; it bowed its grey old head over the fate of its daughter. The people who had been coming were put off; dinner became a ceremony enacted mainly by the servants. I sat alone with Christopher Chantry, whose honest hair, in his mystification, stuck out as if he had been overhauling accounts. My hours with Louisa were even more intensely silent, for she almost never looked at me. In the watches of the night however I at last saw more clearly into what she was thinking of. Once when I caught her wan eyes resting upon me I took advantage of it to kneel down by her bed and speak to her with the utmost tenderness.

"If you can't say it to your mother, can you say it perhaps to *me*?"

She gazed at me for some time. "What does it matter now—if I'm dying?"

I shook my head and smiled. "You won't die if you get it off your mind."

"You'd be cruel to him," she said. "He's innocent—he's innocent."

"Do you mean *you're* guilty? What trifle are you magnifying?"

"Do you call it a trifle———?" She faltered and paused.

"Certainly I do, my dear." Then I risked a great stroke. "I've often done it myself!"

"*You*? Never, never! I was cruel to him," she added.

This puzzled me; I couldn't work it into my conception. "How were you cruel?"

"In the garden. I changed suddenly, I drove him away, I told him he filled me with horror."

"Why did you do that?"

"Because my shame came over me."

"Your shame?"

"What I had done in the house."

"And what had you done?"

She lay a few moments with her eyes closed, as if she were living it over. "I broke out to him, I told him," she began at last. But she couldn't continue, she was powerless to utter it.

"Yes, I know what you told him. Millions of girls have told young men that before."

"They've been asked, they've been asked! They didn't speak *first*! I didn't even know him, he didn't care for me, I had seen him for the first time the day before. I said strange things to him, and he behaved like a gentleman."

"Well he might!"

"Then before he could turn round, when we had simply walked out of the house together and strolled in the garden—it was as if I were borne along in the air by the wonder of what I had said—it rolled over me that I was lost."

"Lost?"

"That I had been horrible—that I had been mad. Nothing could never unsay it. I frightened him—I almost struck him."

"Poor fellow!" I smiled.

"Yes—pity him. He was kind. But he'll see me that way—always!"

I hesitated as to the answer it was best to make to this; then I produced: "Don't think he'll remember you—he'll see other girls."

"Ah, he'll *forget* me!" she softly and miserably wailed; and I saw that I had said the wrong thing. I bent over her more closely, to kiss her, and when I raised my head her mother was on the other side of the bed. She fell on her knees there for the same purpose, and when Louisa felt her lips she stretched out her arms to embrace her. She had the strength to draw her close, and I heard her begin again, for the hundredth time, "Mother, mother——"

"Yes, my own darling."

Then for the hundredth time I heard her stop. There was an intensity in her silence. It made me wildly nervous; I got up and turned away.

"Mother, mother," the girl repeated, and poor Helen replied with a sound of passionate solicitation. But her daughter only exhaled in the waiting hush, while I stood at the window where the dawn was faint, the most miserable moan in the world. "I'm dying," she said, articulately; and she died that night, after an hour, unconscious. The doctor arrived almost at the moment; this time he was sure it must have been the heart. The poor parents were in stupefaction, and I gave up half my visits and stayed with them a month. But in spite of their stupefaction I kept my vow.

COLLABORATION

I don't know how much people care for my work, but they like my studio (of which indeed I am exceedingly fond myself), as they show by their inclination to congregate there at dusky hours on winter afternoons, or on long dim evenings when the place looks well with its rich combinations and low-burning lamps and the bad pictures (my own) are not particularly visible. I won't go into the question of how many of these are purchased, but I rejoice in the distinction that my invitations are never declined. Some of my visitors have been good enough to say that on Sunday evenings in particular there is no pleasanter place in Paris—where so many places are pleasant—none friendlier to easy talk and repeated cigarettes, to the exchange of points of view and the comparison of accents. The air is as international as only Parisian air can be; women, I surmise, think they look well in it; they come also because they fancy they are doing something Bohemian, just as many of the men come because they suppose they are doing something correct. The old heraldic cushions on the divans, embossed with rusty gold, are favourable both to expansion and to contraction—that of course of contracting parties—and the Italian brocade on the walls appeals to one's highest feelings. Music makes its home there—though I confess I am not quite the master of *that* house, and when it is going on in a truly receptive hush I enjoy the way my company leans back and gazes through the thin smoke of cigarettes up at the distant Tiepolo in the almost palatial ceiling. I make sure the piano, the tobacco and the tea are all of the best.

For the conversation, I leave that mostly to take care of itself. There are discussions of course and differences—sometimes even a violent circulation of sense and sound; but I have a consciousness that beauty flourishes and that harmonies prevail in the end. I have occasionally known a visitor to be rude to me because he disliked another visitor's opinions—I had seen an old habitué slip away without bidding me good night on the arrival of some confident specimen of *les jeunes*; but as a general thing we have it out together on the spot—the place is really a chamber of justice, a temple of reconciliation: we understand each other if we only sit up late enough. Art protects her children in the long run—she only asks them to trust her. She is like the Catholic Church—she guarantees paradise to the faithful. Music moreover is a universal solvent; though I've not an infallible ear I've a sufficient sense of the matter for that. Ah, the wounds I've known it to heal—the bridges I've known it to build—the ghosts I've known it to lay! Though I've seen people stalk out I've never observed them not to steal back. My studio in short is the theatre of a cosmopolite drama, a comedy essentially "of character."

One of the liveliest scenes of the performance was the evening, last winter, on which I became aware that one of my compatriots—an American, my good friend Alfred Bonus—was engaged in a controversy somewhat acrimonious, on a literary subject, with Herman Heidenmauer, the young composer who had been playing to us divinely a short time before and whom I thought of neither as a disputant nor as an Englishman. I perceived in a moment that something had happened to present him in this combined character to poor Bonus, who was so ardent a patriot that he lived in Paris rather than in London, who had met his interlocutor for the first time on this occasion, and who apparently had been misled by the perfection with which Heidenmauer spoke English—he spoke it really better than Alfred Bonus. The young musician, a born Bavarian, had spent a few years in England, where he had a commercial step-brother planted and more or less prosperous—a helpful man who had watched over his difficult first steps, given him a temporary home, found him publishers and pupils, smoothed the way to a stupefied hearing for his first productions. He knew his London and might at a first glance have been taken for one of its products; but he had, in addition to a genius of the sort that London fosters but doesn't beget, a very German soul. He brought me a note from an old friend on the other side of the Channel, and I liked him as soon as I looked at him; so much indeed that I could forgive him for making me feel thin and empirical, conscious that *he* was one of the higher kind whom the future has looked in the face. He had met through his gold spectacles her deep eyes, and some mutual communication had occurred. This had given him a confidence which passed for conceit only with those who didn't know the reason.

I guessed the reason early, and, as may be imagined, he didn't grudge me the knowledge. He was happy and various—as little as possible the mere long-haired musicmonger. His hair was short—it was only his legs and his laughter that were long. He was fair and rosy, and his gold spectacles glittered as if in response to the example set them by his beautiful young golden beard. You would have been sure he was an artist without going so far as to decide upon his particular passion; for you would have been conscious that whatever this passion might be it was acquainted with many of the others and mixed with them to its profit. Yet these discoveries had not been fully made by Alfred Bonus, whose occupation was to write letters to the American journals about the way the "boys" were coming on in Paris; for in such a case he probably would not have expected such nebulous greatness to condense at a moment's notice. Bonus is clever and critical, and a sort of self-appointed emissary or agent of the great republic.

He has it at heart to prove that the Americans in Europe *do* get on—taking for granted on the part of the Americans at home an interest in this subject greater, as I often assure him, than any really felt. "Come, now, do *I* get on?" I often ask him; and I sometimes push the inquiry so far as to stammer: "And you, my dear Bonus, do *you* get on?" He is apt to look a little injured on such occasions, as if he would like to say in reply: "Don't you call it success to have Sunday evenings at which I'm a regular attendant? And can you question for a moment the figure I make at them?" It has even occurred to me that he suspects me of painting badly on purpose to spite him—that is to interfere with his favourite dogma. Therefore to spite me in return he's in the heroic predicament of refusing to admit that I'm a failure. He takes a great interest in the plastic arts, but his intensest sympathy is for literature. This sentiment is somewhat starved, as in that school the boys languish as yet on a back seat. To show what they are doing Bonus has to retreat upon the studios, but there is nothing he enjoys so much as having, when the rare chance offers, a good literary talk. He follows the French movement closely and explains it profusely to our compatriots, whom he mystifies, but who guess he's rather loose.

I forget how his conversation with Heidenmauer began—it was, I think, some difference of opinion about one of the English poets that set them afloat. Heidenmauer knows the English poets, and the French, and the Italian, and the Spanish, and the Russian—he is a wonderful representative of that Germanism which consists in the negation of intellectual frontiers. It is the English poets that, if I'm not mistaken, he loves best, and probably the harm was done by his having happened to say so. At any rate Alfred Bonus let him have it, without due notice perhaps, which is rather Alfred's way, on the question (a favourite one with my compatriot) of the backward state of literature in England, for which after all Heidenmauer was not responsible. Bonus believes in responsibility—the responsibility of others, an attitude which tends to make some of his friends extremely secretive, though perhaps it would have been justified—as to this I'm not sure—had Heidenmauer been, under the circumstances, technically British. Before he had had time to explain that he was not, the other persons present had become aware that a kind of challenge had passed—that nation, in a sudden startled flurry, somehow found itself pitted against nation. There was much vagueness at first as to which of the nations were engaged and as to what their quarrel was about, the question coming presently to appear less simple than the spectacle (so easily conceivable) of a German's finding it hot for him in a French house, a house French enough at any rate to give countenance to the idea of his quick defeat.

How could the right cause fail of protection in any house of which Madame de Brindes and her charming daughter were so good as to be assiduous frequenters? I recollect perfectly the pale gleam of joy in the mother's handsome face when she gathered that what had happened was that a detested German was on his defence. She wears her eternal mourning (I admit it's immensely becoming) for a triple woe, for multiplied griefs and wrongs, all springing from the crash of the Empire, from the battlefields of 1870. Her husband fell at Sedan, her father and her brother on still darker days; both her own family and that of M. de Brindes, their general situation in life, were, as may be said, creations of the Empire, so that from one hour to the other she found herself sinking with the wreck. You won't recognise her under the name I give her, but you may none the less have admired, between their pretty lemon-coloured covers, the touching tales of Claude Lorrain. She plies an ingenious, pathetic pen and has reconciled herself to effort and privation for the sake of her daughter. I say privation, because these distinguished women are poor, receive with great modesty and have broken with a hundred of those social sanctities than are dearer to French souls than to any others. They have gone down into the market-place, and Paule de Brindes, who is three-and-twenty to-day and has a happy turn for keeping a water-colour liquid, earns a hundred francs here and there. She is not so handsome as her mother, but she has magnificent hair and what the French call a look of race, and is, or at least was till the other day, a frank and charming young woman. There is something exquisite in the way these ladies are earnestly, conscientiously modern. From the moment they accept necessities they accept them all, and poor Madame de Brindes flatters herself that she has made her dowerless daughter one of us others. The girl goes out alone, talks with young men and, although she only paints landscape, takes a free view of the *convenances*. Nothing can please either of them more than to tell them they have thrown over their superstitions. They haven't, thank heaven; and when I want to be reminded of some of the prettiest in the world—of a thousand fine scruples and pleasant forms, and of what grace can do for the sake of grace—I know where to go for it.

It was a part of this pious heresy—much more august in the way they presented it than some of the aspects of the old faith—that Paule should have become "engaged," quite like a *jeune mees*, to my brilliant friend Félix Vendemer. He is such a votary of the modern that he was inevitably interested in the girl of the future and had matched one reform with another, being ready to marry without a penny, as the clearest way of expressing his appreciation, this favourable specimen of the type. He simply fell in love with Mademoiselle de Brindes and behaved, on his side, equally like one of us others, except that he begged me to ask her mother for her hand. I was inspired to do so with eloquence, and my friends were not insensible of such an opportunity to show that they now lived in the world of realities. Vendemer's sole fortune is his genius, and he and Paule, who confessed to an answering flame, plighted their troth like a pair of young rustics or (what comes for French people to the same thing) young Anglo-Saxons. Madame de Brindes thinks such doings at bottom very vulgar; but vulgar is what she tries hard to be, she is so convinced it is the only way to make a living. Vendemer had had at that time only the first of his successes, which was not, as you will remember—and unfortunately for Madame de Brindes—of this remunerative kind. Only a few people recognised the perfection of his little volume of verse: my acquaintance with him originated in my having been one of the few. A volume of verse was a scanty provision to marry on, so that, still like a pair of us others, the luckless lovers had to bide their time. Presently however came the success (again a success only with those who care for quality, not with the rough and ready public) of his comedy in verse at the Français. This charming work had just been taken off (it had been found not to make money), when the various parties to my little drama met Heidenmauer at my studio.

Vendemer, who has, as indeed the others have, a passion for music, was tremendously affected by hearing him play two or three of his compositions, and I immediately saw that the immitigable German quality was a morsel much less bitter for him than for the two uncompromising ladies. He went so far as to speak to Heidenmauer frankly, to thank him with effusion, an effort of which neither of the quivering women would have been capable. Vendemer was in the room the night Alfred Bonus raised his little breeze; I saw him lean on the piano and listen with a queer face looking however rather wonderingly at Heidenmauer. Before this I had noticed the instant paleness (her face was admirably expressive) with which Madame de Brindes saw her prospective son-in-law make up, as it were, to the original Teuton, whose national character was intensified to her aching mind, as it would have been to that of most Frenchwomen in her place, by his wash of English colour. A German was bad enough—but a German with English aggravations! Her senses were too fine to give her the excuse of not feeling that his compositions were interesting, and she was capable, magnanimously, of listening to them with dropped eyes; but (much as it ever cost her not to be perfectly courteous), she couldn't have made even the most superficial speech to him about them. Marie de Brindes could never have spoken to Herman Heidenmauer. It was a narrowness if you will, but a narrowness that to my vision was enveloped in a dense atmosphere—a kind of sunset bloom—of enriching and fortifying things. Herman Heidenmauer himself, like the man of imagination and the lover of life that he was, would have entered into it delightedly, been charmed with it as a fine case of bigotry. This was conspicuous in Marie de Brindes: her loyalty to the national idea was that of a *dévote* to a form of worship. She never spoke of France, but she always made me think of it, and with an authority which the women of her race seem to me to have in the question much more than the men. I dare say I'm rather in love with her, though, being considerably younger, I've never told her so—as if she would in the least mind that! I have indeed been a little checked by a spirit of allegiance to Vendemer; suspecting always (excuse my sophistication) that in the last analysis it is the mother's charm that he feels—or originally felt—in the daughter's. He spoke of the elder lady to me in those days with the insistence with which only a Frenchman can speak of the objects of his affection. At any rate there was always something symbolic and slightly ceremonial to me in her delicate cameo-face and her general black-robed presence: she made me think of a priestess or a mourner, of revolutions and sieges, detested treaties and ugly public things. I pitied her, too, for the strife of the elements in her—for the way she must have felt a noble enjoyment mutilated. She was too good for that, and yet she was too rigid for anything else; and the sight of such dismal perversions made me hate more than ever the stupid terms on which nations have organised their intercourse.

When she gathered that one of my guests was simply cramming it down the throat of another that the English literary mind was not even literary, she turned away with a vague shrug and a pitiful look at her daughter for the taste of people who took their pleasure so poorly: the truth in question would be so obvious that it was not worth making a scene about. Madame de Brindes evidently looked at any scene between the English and the Americans as a quarrel proceeding vaguely from below stairs—a squabble sordidly domestic. Her almost immediate departure with her daughter operated as a lucky interruption, and I caught for the first time in the straight, spare girl, as she followed her mother, a little of the air that Vendemer had told me he found in her, the still exaltation, the brown uplifted head that we attribute, or that at any rate he made it visible to me that he attributed, to the dedicated Maid. He considered that his intended bore a striking resemblance to Jeanne d'Arc, and he marched after her on this occasion like a square-shouldered armour-bearer. He reappeared, however, after he had put the ladies into a cab, and half an hour later the rest of my friends, with the sole exception of Bonus, having dispersed, he was sitting up with me in the empty studio for another *bout de causerie*. At first perhaps I was too occupied with reprimanding my compatriot to give much attention to what Vendemer might have to say; I remember at any rate that I had asked Bonus what had induced him to make so grave a blunder. He was not even yet, it appeared, aware of his blunder, so that I had to inquire by what odd chance he had taken Heidenmauer for a bigoted Briton.

"If I spoke to him as one he answered as one; that's bigoted enough," said Alfred Bonus.

"He was confused and amused at your onslaught: he wondered what fly had stung you."

"The fly of patriotism," Vendemer suggested.

"Do *you* like him—a beast of a German?" Bonus demanded.

"If he's an Englishman he isn't a German—*il faut opter*. We can hang him for the one or for the other, we can't hang him for both. I was immensely struck with those things he played."

"They had no charm for me, or doubtless I too should have been demoralised," Alfred said. "He seemed to know nothing about Miss Brownrigg. Now Miss Brownrigg's great."

"I like the things and even the people you quarrel about, you big babies of the same breast. *C'est à se tordre!*" Vendemer declared.

"I may be very abject, but I *do* take an interest in the American novel," Alfred rejoined.

"I hate such expressions: there's no such thing as the American novel."

"Is there by chance any such thing as the French?"

"*Pas davantage*—for the artist himself: how can you ask? I don't know what is meant by French art and English art and American art: those seem to me mere cataloguers' and reviewers' and tradesmen's names, representing preoccupations utterly foreign to the artist. Art is art in every country, and the novel (since Bonus mentions that) is the novel in every tongue, and hard enough work they have to live up to that privilege, without our adding another muddle to the problem. The reader, the consumer may call things as he likes, but we leave him to his little amusements." I suggested that we were all readers and consumers; which only made Vendemer continue: "Yes, and only a small handful of us have the ghost of a palate. But you and I and Bonus are of the handful."

"What do you mean by the handful?" Bonus inquired.

Vendemer hesitated a moment. "I mean the few intelligent people, and even the few people who are not——" He paused again an instant, long enough for me to request him not to say what they were "not," and then went on: "People in a word who have the honour to live in the only country worth living in."

"And pray what country is that?"

"The land of dreams—the country of art."

"Oh, the land of dreams! I live in the land of realities!" Bonus exclaimed. "What do you all mean then by chattering so about *le roman russe?*"

"It's a convenience—to identify the work of three or four, *là-bas*, because we're so far from it. But do you see them *writing* 'le roman russe?'"

"I happen to know that that's exactly what they want to do, some of them," said Bonus.

"Some of the idiots, then! There are plenty of those everywhere. Anything born under that silly star is sure not to count."

"Thank God I'm not an artist!" said Bonus.

"Dear Alfred's a critic," I explained.

"And I'm not ashamed of my country," he subjoined.

"Even a critic perhaps may be an artist," Vendemer mused.

"Then as the great American critic Bonus may be the great American artist," I went on.

"Is that what you're supposed to give us—'American' criticism?" Vendemer asked, with dismay in his expressive, ironic face. "Take care, take care, or it will be more American than critical, and then where will *you* be? However," he continued, laughing and with a change of tone, "I may see the matter in too lurid a light, for I've just been favoured with a judgment conceived in the purest spirit of our own national genius." He looked at me a moment and then he remarked: "That dear Madame de Brindes doesn't approve of my attitude."

"Your attitude?"

"Toward your German friend. She let me know it when I went down stairs with her—told me I was much too cordial, that I must observe myself."

"And what did you reply to that?"

"I answered that the things he had played were extraordinarily beautiful."

"And how did she meet that?"

"By saying that he's an enemy of our country."

"She had you there," I rejoined.

"Yes, I could only reply '*Chère madame, voyons!*'"

"That was meagre."

"Evidently, for it did no more for me than to give her a chance to declare that he can't possibly be here for any good and that he belongs to a race it's my sacred duty to loathe."

"I see what she means."

"I don't then—where artists are concerned. I said to her: '*Ah, madame, vous savez que pour moi il n'y a que l'art!*'"

"It's very exciting!" I laughed. "How could she parry that?"

"'I know it, my dear child—but for *him*?' That's the way she parried it. 'Very well, for him?' I asked. 'For him there's the insolence of the victor and a secret scorn for our incurable illusions!'"

"Heidenmauer has no insolence and no secret scorn."

Vendemer was silent a moment. "Are you very sure of that?"

"Oh, I like him! He's out of all that, and far above it. But what did Mademoiselle Paule say?" I inquired.

"She said nothing—she only looked at me."

"Happy man!"

"Not a bit. She looked at me with strange eyes, in which I could read 'Go straight, my friend—go straight!' *Oh, les femmes, les femmes!*"

"What's the matter with them now?"

"They've a mortal hatred of art!"

"It's a true, deep instinct," said Alfred Bonus.

"But what passed further with Madame de Brindes?" I went on.

"She only got into her cab, pushing her daughter first; on which I slammed the door rather hard and came up here. *Cela m'a porté sur les nerfs.*"

"I'm afraid I haven't soothed them," Bonus said, looking for his hat. When he had found it he added: "When the English have beaten us and pocketed our *milliards* I'll forgive them; but not till then!" And with this he went off, made a little uncomfortable, I think, by Vendemer's sharper alternatives, while the young Frenchman called after him: "My dear fellow, at night all cats are grey!"

Vendemer, when we were left alone together, mooned about the empty studio awhile and asked me three or four questions about Heidenmauer. I satisfied his curiosity as well as I could, but I demanded the reason of it. The reason he gave was that one of the young German's compositions had already begun to haunt his memory; but that was a reason which, to my sense, still left something unexplained. I didn't however challenge him, before he quitted me, further than to warn him against being deliberately perverse.

"What do you mean by being deliberately perverse?" He fixed me so with his intensely living French eye that I became almost blushingly conscious of a certain insincerity and, instead of telling him what I meant, tried to get off with the deplorable remark that the prejudices of Mesdames de Brindes were after all respectable. "That's exactly what makes them so odious!" cried Vendemer.

A few days after this, late in the afternoon, Herman Heidenmauer came in to see me and found the young Frenchman seated at my piano—trying to win back from the keys some echo of a passage in the *Abendlied* we had listened to on the Sunday evening. They met, naturally, as good friends, and Heidenmauer sat down with instant readiness and gave him again the page he was trying to recover. He asked him for his address, that he might send him the composition, and at Vendemer's request, as we sat in the firelight, played half-a-dozen other things. Vendemer listened in silence but to my surprise took leave of me before the lamp was brought in. I asked him to stay to dinner (I had already appealed to Heidenmauer to stay), but he explained that he was engaged to dine with Madame de Brindes—*à la maison* as he always called it. When he had gone Heidenmauer, with whom on departing he had shaken hands without a word, put to me the same questions about him that Vendemer had asked on the Sunday evening about the young German, and I replied that my visitor would find in a small volume of remarkable verse published by Lemerre, which I placed in his hands, much of the information he desired. This volume, which had just appeared, contained, beside a reprint of Vendemer's earlier productions, many of them admirable lyrics, the drama that had lately been played at the Français, and Heidenmauer took it with him when he left me. But he left me late, and before this occurred, all the evening, we had much talk about the French nation. In the foreign colony of Paris the exchange of opinions on this subject is one of the most inevitable and by no means the least interesting of distractions; it furnishes occupation to people rather conscious of the burden of leisure. Heidenmauer had been little in Paris, but he was all the more open to impressions; they evidently poured in upon him and he gave them a generous hospitality. In the diffused white light of his fine German intelligence old colours took on new tints to me, and while we spun fancies about the wonderful race around us I added to my little stock of notions about his own. I saw that his admiration for our neighbours was a very high tide, and I was struck with something bland and unconscious (noble and serene in its absence of precautions) in the way he let his doors stand open to it. It would have been exasperating to many

Frenchmen; he looked at them through his clear spectacles with such an absence of suspicion that they might have anything to forgive him, such a thin metaphysical view of instincts and passions. He had the air of not allowing for recollections and nerves, and would doubtless give them occasion to make afresh some of their reflections on the tact of *ces gens-là*.

A couple of days after I had given him Vendemer's book he came back to tell me that he found great beauty in it. "It speaks to me—it speaks to me," he said with his air of happy proof. "I liked the songs—I liked the songs. Besides," he added, "I like the little romantic play—it has given me wonderful ideas; more ideas than anything has done for a long time. Yes—yes."

"What kind of ideas?"

"Well, this kind." And he sat down to the piano and struck the keys. I listened without more questions, and after a while I began to understand. Suddenly he said: "Do you know the words of *that*?" and before I could answer he was rolling out one of the lyrics of the little volume. The poem was strange and obscure, yet irresistibly beautiful, and he had translated it into music still more tantalizing than itself. He sounded the words with his German accent, barely perceptible in English but strongly marked in French. He dropped them and took them up again; he was playing with them, feeling his way. "*This* is my idea!" he broke out; he had caught it, in one of its mystic mazes, and he rendered it with a kind of solemn freshness. There was a phrase he repeated, trying it again and again, and while he did so he chanted the words of the song as if they were an illuminating flame, an inspiration. I was rather glad on the whole that Vendemer didn't hear what his pronunciation made of them, but as I was in the very act of rejoicing I became aware that the author of the verses had opened the door. He had pushed it gently, hearing the music; then hearing also his own poetry he had paused and stood looking at Heidenmauer. The young German nodded and laughed and, irreflectively, spontaneously, greeted him with a friendly "*Was sagen Sie dazu?*" I saw Vendemer change colour; he blushed red and, for an instant, as he stood wavering, I thought he was going to retreat. But I beckoned him in and, on the divan beside me, patted a place for him to sit.

He came in but didn't take this place; he went and stood before the fire to warm his feet, turning his back to us. Heidenmauer played and played, and after a little Vendemer turned round; he looked about him for a seat, dropped into it and sat with his elbows on his knees and his head in his hands. Presently Heidenmauer called out, in French, above the music: "I like your songs—I like them immensely!" but the young Frenchman neither spoke nor moved. When however five minutes later Heidenmauer stopped he sprang up with an entreaty to him to go on, to go on for the love of God. "*Foilà—foilà!*" cried the musician, and with hands for an instant suspended he wandered off into mysterious worlds. He played Wagner and then Wagner again—a great deal of Wagner; in the midst of which, abruptly, he addressed himself again to Vendemer, who had gone still further from the piano, launching to me, however from his corner a "*Dieu, que c'est beau!*" which I saw that Heidenmauer caught. "I've a conception for an opera, you know—I'd give anything if you'd do the libretto!" Our German friend laughed out, after this, with clear good nature, and the rich appeal brought Vendemer slowly to his feet again, staring at the musician across the room and turning this time perceptibly pale.

I felt there was a drama in the air, and it made me a little nervous; to conceal which I said to Heidenmauer: "What's your conception? What's your subject?"

"My conception would be realized in the subject of M. Vendemer's play—if he'll do that for me in a great lyric manner!" And with this the young German, who had stopped playing to answer me, quitted the piano and Vendemer got up to meet him. "The subject is splendid—it has taken possession of me. Will you do it with me? Will you work with me? We shall make something great!"

"Ah, you don't know what you ask!" Vendemer answered, with his pale smile.

"I do—I do: I've thought of it. It will be bad for me in my country; I shall suffer for it. They won't like it—they'll abuse me for it—they'll say of me *pis que pendre*." Heidenmauer pronounced it *bis que bendre.*

"They'll hate my libretto so?" Vendemer asked.

"Yes, your libretto—they'll say it's immoral and horrible. And they'll say *I'm* immoral and horrible for having worked with you," the young composer went on, with his pleasant healthy lucidity. "You'll injure my career. Oh yes, I shall suffer!" he joyously, exultingly cried.

"*Et moi donc!*" Vendemer exclaimed.

"Public opinion, yes. I shall also make you suffer—I shall nip your prosperity in the bud. All that's *des bêtises—tes pétisses*," said poor Heidenmauer. "In art there are no countries."

"Yes, art is terrible, art is monstrous," Vendemer replied, looking at the fire.

"I love your songs—they have extraordinary beauty."

"And Vendemer has an equal taste for your compositions," I said to Heidenmauer.

"Tempter!" Vendemer murmured to me, with a strange look.

"*C'est juste!* I mustn't meddle—which will be all the easier as I'm dining out and must go and dress. You two make yourselves at home and fight it out here."

"Do you *leave* me?" asked Vendemer, still with his strange look.

"My dear fellow, I've only just time."

"We will dine together—he and I—at one of those characteristic places, and we will look at the matter in its different relations," said Heidenmauer. "Then we will come back here to finish—your studio is so good for music."

"There are some things it *isn't* good for," Vendemer remarked, looking at our companion.

"It's good for poetry—it's good for truth," smiled the composer.

"You'll stay *here* and dine together," I said; "my servant can manage that."

"No, no—we'll go out and we'll walk together. We'll talk a great deal," Heidenmauer went on. "The subject is so comprehensive," he said to Vendemer, as he lighted another cigar.

"The subject?"

"Of your drama. It's so universal."

"Ah, the universe—*il n'y a que ça!*" I laughed, to Vendemer, partly with a really amused sense of the exaggerated woe that looked out of his poetic eyes and that seemed an appeal to me not to forsake him, to throw myself into the scale of the associations he would have to stifle, and partly to encourage him, to express my conviction that two such fine minds couldn't in the long run be the worse for coming to an agreement. I might have been a more mocking Mephistopheles handing over his pure spirit to my literally German Faust.

When I came home at eleven o'clock I found him alone in my studio, where, evidently, for some time, he had been moving up and down in agitated thought. The air was thick with Bavarian fumes, with the reverberation of mighty music and great ideas, with the echoes of that "universe" to which I had so mercilessly consigned him. But I judged in a moment that Vendemer was in a very different phase of his evolution from the one in which I had left him. I had never seen his handsome, sensitive face so intensely illumined.

"*Ça y est—ça y est!*" he exclaimed, standing there with his hands in his pockets and looking at me.

"You've really agreed to do something together?"

"We've sworn a tremendous oath—we've taken a sacred engagement."

"My dear fellow, you're a hero."

"Wait and see! *C'est un très-grand esprit.*"

"So much the better!"

"*C'est un bien beau génie.* Ah, we've risen—we soar; *nous sommes dans les grandes espaces!*" my friend continued with his dilated eyes.

"It's very interesting—because it will cost you something."

"It will cost me everything!" said Félix Vendemer in a tone I seem to hear at this hour. "That's just the beauty of it. It's the chance of chances to testify for art—to affirm an indispensable truth."

"An indispensable truth?" I repeated, feeling myself soar too, but into the splendid vague.

"Do you know the greatest crime that can be perpetrated against it?"

"Against it?" I asked, still soaring.

"Against the religion of art—against the love for beauty—against the search for the Holy Grail?" The transfigured look with which he named these things, the way his warm voice filled the rich room, was a revelation of the wonderful talk that had taken place.

"Do you know—for one of *us*—the really damnable, the only unpardonable, sin?"

"Tell me, so that I may keep clear of it!"

"To profane *our* golden air with the hideous invention of patriotism."

"It was a clever invention in its time!" I laughed.

"I'm not talking about its time—I'm talking about, its place. It was never anything but a fifth-rate impertinence here. In art there are no countries—no idiotic nationalities, no frontiers, nor *douanes*, nor still more idiotic fortresses and bayonets. It has the unspeakable beauty of being the region in which those abominations cease, the medium in which such vulgarities simply can't live. What therefore are we to say of the brutes who wish to drag them all in—to crush to death with them all the flowers of such a garden, to shut out all the light of such a sky?" I was far from desiring to defend the "brutes" in question, though there rose before me even at that moment a sufficiently vivid picture of the way, later on, poor Vendemer would have to face them. I quickly perceived indeed that the picture was, to his own eyes, a still more crowded canvas. Félix Vendemer, in the centre of it, was an admirable, a really sublime figure. If there had been wonderful talk after I quitted the two poets the wonder was not over yet—it went on far into the night for my benefit. We looked at the prospect in many lights, turned the subject about almost every way it would go; but I am bound to say there was one relation in which we tacitly agreed to forbear to consider it. We neither of us uttered the name of Paule de Brindes—the outlook in that direction would too serious. And yet if Félix Vendemer, exquisite and incorruptible artist that he was, had fallen in love with the idea of "testifying," it was from that direction that the finest part of his opportunity to do so would proceed.

I was only too conscious of this when, within the week, I received a hurried note from Madame de Brindes, begging me as a particular favour to come and see her without delay. I had not seen Vendemer again, but I had had a characteristic call from Heidenmauer, who, though I could imagine him perfectly in a Prussian helmet, with a needle-gun, perfectly, on definite occasion, a sturdy, formidable soldier, gave me a renewed impression of inhabiting, in the expansion of his genius and the exercise of his intelligence, no land of red tape, no province smaller nor more pedantically administered than the totality of things. I was reminded afresh too that *he* foresaw no striking salon-picture, no *chic* of execution nor romance of martyrdom, or at any rate devoted very little time to the consideration of such objects. He doubtless did scant justice to poor Vendemer's attitude, though he said to me of him by the way, with his rosy deliberation: "He has good ideas—he has good ideas. The French mind has—for me—the taste of a very delightful *bonbon*!" He only measured the angle of convergence, as he called it, of their two projections. He was in short not preoccupied with the personal gallantry of their experiment; he was preoccupied with its "æsthetic and harmonic basis."

It was without her daughter that Madame de Brindes received me, when I obeyed her summons, in her scrap of a *quatrième* in the Rue de Miromesnil.

"Ah, *cher monsieur*, how could you have permitted such a horror—how could you have given it the countenance of your roof, of your influence?" There were tears in her eyes, and I don't think that for the moment I have ever been more touched by a reproach. But I pulled myself together sufficiently to affirm my faith as well as to disengage my responsibility. I explained that there was no horror to me in the matter, that if I was not a German neither was I a Frenchman, and that all I had before me was two young men inflamed by a great idea and nobly determined to work together to give it a great form.

"A great idea—to go over to *ces gens-là?*"

"To go over to them?"

"To put yourself on their side—to throw yourself into the arms of those who hate us—to fall into their abominable trap!"

"What do you call their abominable trap?"

"Their false *bonhomie*, the very impudence of their intrigues, their profound, scientific deceit and their determination to get the advantage of us by exploiting our generosity."

"You attribute to such a man as Heidenmauer too many motives and too many calculations. He's quite ideally superior!"

"Oh, German idealism—we know what that means! We've no use for their superiority; let them carry it elsewhere—let them leave us alone. Why do they thrust themselves in upon us and set old wounds throbbing by their detested presence? We don't go near *them*, or ever wish to hear their ugly names or behold their *visages de bois*; therefore the most rudimentary good taste, the tact one would expect even from naked savages, might suggest to them to seek their amusements elsewhere. But *their* taste, *their* tact—I can scarcely trust myself to speak!"

Madame de Brindes did speak however at considerable further length and with a sincerity of passion which left one quite without arguments. There was no argument to meet the fact that Vendemer's attitude wounded her, wounded her daughter, *jusqu'au fond de l'âme*, that it represented for them abysses of shame and suffering and that for himself it meant a whole future compromised, a whole public alienated. It was vain doubtless to talk of such things; if people didn't *feel* them, if they hadn't the fibre of loyalty, the high imagination of honour, all explanations, all supplications were but a waste of noble emotion. M. Vendemer's perversity was monstrous—she had had a sickening discussion with him. What she desired of me was to make one last appeal to him, to put the solemn truth before him, to try to bring him back to sanity. It was as if he had temporarily lost his reason. It was to be made clear to him, *par exemple*, that unless he should recover it Mademoiselle de Brindes would unhesitatingly withdraw from her engagement.

"Does she *really* feel as you do?" I asked.

"Do you think I put words into her mouth? She feels as a *fille de France* is obliged to feel!"

"Doesn't she love him then?"

"She adores him. But she won't take him without his honour."

"I don't understand such refinements!" I said.

"Oh, *vous autres!*" cried Madame de Brindes. Then with eyes glowing through her tears she demanded: "Don't you know she knows how her father died?" I was on the point of saying "What has that to do with it?" but I withheld the question, for after all I could conceive that it might have something. There was no disputing about tastes, and I could only express my sincere conviction that Vendemer was profoundly attached to Mademoiselle Paule. "Then let him prove it by making her a sacrifice!" my strenuous hostess replied; to which I rejoined that I would repeat our conversation to him and put the matter before him as strongly as I could. I delayed a little to take leave, wondering if the girl would not come in—I should have been so much more content to receive her strange recantation from her own lips. I couldn't say this to Madame de Brindes; but she guessed I meant it, and before we separated we exchanged a look in which our mutual mistrust was written—the suspicion on her side that I should not be a very passionate intercessor and the conjecture on mine that she might be misrepresenting her daughter. This slight tension, I must add, was only momentary, for I have had a chance of observing Paule de Brindes since then, and the two ladies were soon satisfied that I pitied them enough to have been eloquent.

My eloquence has been of no avail, and I have learned (it has been one of the most interesting lessons of my life) of what transcendent stuff the artist may sometimes be made. Herman Heidenmauer and Félix Vendemer are, at the hour I write, immersed in their monstrous collaboration. There were postponements and difficulties at first, and there will be more serious ones in the future, when it is a question of giving the finished work to the world. The world of Paris will stop its ears in horror, the German Empire will turn its mighty back, and the authors of what I foresee (oh, I've been treated to specimens!) as a perhaps really epoch-making musical revelation (is Heidenmauer's style rubbing off on me?) will perhaps have to beg for a hearing in communities fatally unintelligent. It may very well be that they will not obtain any hearing at all for years. I like at any rate to think that time works for them. At present they work for themselves and for each other, amid drawbacks of several kinds. Separating after the episode in Paris, they have met again on alien soil, at a little place on the Genoese Riviera where sunshine is cheap and tobacco bad, and they live (the two together) for five francs a day, which is all they can muster between them. It appears that when Heidenmauer's London step-brother was informed of the young composer's unnatural alliance he instantly withdrew his subsidy. The return of it is contingent on the rupture of the unholy union and the destruction by flame of all the manuscript. The pair are very poor and the whole thing depends on their staying power. They are so preoccupied with their opera that they have no time for pot-boilers. Vendemer is in a feverish hurry, lest perhaps he should find himself chilled. There are still other details which contribute to the interest of the episode and which, for me, help to render it a most refreshing, a really great little case. It rests me, it delights me, there is something in it that makes for civilization. In their way they are working for human happiness. The strange course taken by Vendemer (I mean his renunciation of his engagement) must moreover be judged in the light of the fact that he was really in love. Something had to be sacrificed, and what he clung to most (he's extraordinary, I admit) was the truth he had the opportunity of proclaiming. Men give up their love for advantages every day, but they rarely give it up for such discomforts.

Paule de Brindes was the less in love of the two; I see her often enough to have made up my mind about that. But she's mysterious, she's odd; there was at any rate a sufficient wrench in her life to make her often absent-minded. Does her imagination hover about Félix Vendemer? A month ago, going into their rooms one day when her mother was not at home (the *bonne* had admitted me under a wrong impression) I found her at the piano, playing one of Heidenmauer's compositions—playing it without notes and with infinite expression. How had she got hold of it? How had she learned it? This was her secret—she blushed so that I didn't pry into it. But what is she doing, under the singular circumstances, with a composition of Herman Heidenmauer's? She never met him, she never heard him play but that once. It will be a pretty complication if it shall appear that the young German genius made on that occasion more than one intense impression. This needn't appear, however, inasmuch as, being naturally in terror of the discovery by her mother of such an anomaly, she may count on me absolutely not to betray her. I hadn't fully perceived how deeply susceptible she is to music. She must have a strange confusion of feelings—a dim, haunting trouble, with a kind of ache of impatience for the wonderful opera somewhere in the depths of it. Don't we live fast after all, and doesn't the old order change? Don't say art isn't mighty! I shall give you some more illustrations of it yet.

OWEN WINGRAVE

I

"Upon my honour you must be off your head!" cried Spencer Coyle, as the young man, with a white face, stood there panting a little and repeating "Really, I've quite decided," and "I assure you I've thought it all out." They were both pale, but Owen Wingrave smiled in a manner exasperating to his interlocutor, who however still discriminated sufficiently to see that his grimace (it was like an irrelevant leer) was the result of extreme and conceivable nervousness.

"It was certainly a mistake to have gone so far; but that is exactly why I feel I mustn't go further," poor Owen said, waiting mechanically, almost humbly (he wished not to swagger, and indeed he had nothing to swagger about) and carrying through the window to the stupid opposite houses the dry glitter of his eyes.

"I'm unspeakably disgusted. You've made me dreadfully ill," Mr. Coyle went on, looking thoroughly upset.

"I'm very sorry. It was the fear of the effect on you that kept me from speaking sooner."

"You should have spoken three months ago. Don't you know your mind from one day to the other?"

The young man for a moment said nothing. Then he replied with a little tremor: "You're very angry with me, and I expected it. I'm awfully obliged to you for all you've done for me. I'll do anything else for you in return, but I can't do that. Everyone else will let me have it, of course. I'm prepared for it—I'm prepared for everything. That's what has taken the time: to be sure I was prepared. I think it's your displeasure I feel most and regret most. But little by little you'll get over it."

"*You'll* get over it rather faster, I suppose!" Spencer Coyle satirically exclaimed. He was quite as agitated as his young friend, and they were evidently in no condition to prolong an encounter in which they each drew blood. Mr. Coyle was a professional "coach"; he prepared young men for the army, taking only three or four at a time, to whom he applied the irresistible stimulus of which the possession was both his secret and his fortune. He had not a great establishment; he would have said himself that it was not a wholesale business. Neither his system, his health nor his temper could have accommodated itself to numbers; so he weighed and measured his pupils and turned away more applicants than he passed. He was an artist in his line, caring only for picked subjects and capable of sacrifices almost passionate for the individual. He liked ardent young men (there were kinds of capacity to which he was indifferent) and he had taken a particular fancy to Owen Wingrave. This young man's facility really fascinated him. His candidates usually did wonders, and he might have sent up a multitude. He was a person of exactly the stature of the great Napoleon, with a certain flicker of genius in his light blue eye: it had been said of him that he looked like a pianist. The tone of his favourite pupil now expressed, without intention indeed, a superior wisdom which irritated him. He had not especially suffered before from Wingrave's high opinion of himself, which had seemed justified by remarkable parts; but to-day it struck him as intolerable. He cut short the discussion, declining absolutely to regard their relations as terminated, and remarked to his pupil that he had better go off somewhere (down to Eastbourne, say; the sea would bring him round) and take a few days to find his feet and come to his senses. He could afford the time, he was so well up: when Spencer Coyle remembered how well up he was he could have boxed his ears. The tall, athletic young man was not physically a subject for simplified reasoning; but there was a troubled gentleness in his handsome face, the index of compunction mixed with pertinacity, which signified that if it could have done any good he would have turned both cheeks. He evidently didn't pretend that his wisdom was superior; he only presented it as his own. It was his own career after all that was in question. He couldn't refuse to go through the form of trying Eastbourne or at least of holding his tongue, though there was that in his manner which implied that if he should do so it would be really to give Mr. Coyle a chance to recuperate. He didn't feel a bit overworked, but there was nothing more natural than that with their tremendous pressure Mr. Coyle should be. Mr. Coyle's own intellect would derive an advantage from his pupil's holiday. Mr. Coyle saw what he meant, but he controlled himself; he only demanded, as his right, a truce of three days. Owen Wingrave granted it, though as fostering sad illusions this went visibly against his conscience; but before they separated the famous crammer remarked:

"All the same I feel as if I ought to see someone. I think you mentioned to me that your aunt had come to town?"

"Oh yes; she's in Baker Street. Do go and see her," the boy said comfortingly.

Mr. Coyle looked at him an instant. "Have you broached this folly to her?"

"Not yet—to no one. I thought it right to speak to you first."

"Oh, what you 'think right'!" cried Spencer Coyle, outraged by his young friend's standards. He added that he would probably call on Miss Wingrave; after which the recreant youth got out of the house.

Owen Wingrave didn't however start punctually for Eastbourne; he only directed his steps to Kensington Gardens, from which Mr. Coyle's desirable residence (he was terribly expensive and had a big house) was not far removed. The famous coach "put up" his pupils, and Owen had mentioned to the butler that he would be back to dinner. The spring day was warm to his young blood, and he had a book in his pocket which, when he had passed into the gardens and, after a short stroll, dropped into a chair, he took out with the slow, soft sigh that finally ushers in a pleasure postponed. He stretched his long legs and began to read it; it was a volume of Goethe's poems. He had been for days in a state of the highest tension, and now that the cord had snapped the relief was proportionate; only it was characteristic of him that this deliverance should take the form of an intellectual pleasure. If he had thrown up the probability of a magnificent career it was not to dawdle along Bond Street nor parade his indifference in the window of a club. At any rate he had in a few moments forgotten everything—the tremendous pressure, Mr. Coyle's disappointment, and even his formidable aunt in Baker Street. If these watchers had overtaken him there would surely have been some excuse for their exasperation. There was no doubt he was perverse, for his very choice of a pastime only showed how he had got up his German.

"What the devil's the matter with him, do *you* know?" Spencer Coyle asked that afternoon of young Lechmere, who had never before observed the head of the establishment to set a fellow such an example of bad language. Young Lechmere was not only Wingrave's fellow-pupil, he was supposed to be his intimate, indeed quite his best friend, and had unconsciously performed for Mr. Coyle the office of making the promise of his great gifts more vivid by contrast. He was short and sturdy and as a general thing uninspired, and Mr. Coyle, who found no amusement in believing in him, had never thought him less exciting than as he stared now out of a face from which you could never guess whether he had caught an idea. Young Lechmere concealed such achievements as if they had been youthful indiscretions. At any rate he could evidently conceive no reason why it should be thought there was anything more than usual the matter with the companion of his studies; so Mr. Coyle had to continue:

"He declines to go up. He chucks the whole thing!"

The first thing that struck young Lechmere in the case was the freshness it had imparted to the governor's vocabulary.

"He doesn't want to go to Sandhurst?"

"He doesn't want to go anywhere. He gives up the army altogether. He objects," said Mr. Coyle, in a tone that made young Lechmere almost hold his breath, "to the military profession."

"Why, it has been the profession of all his family!"

"Their profession? It has been their religion! Do you know Miss Wingrave?"

"Oh, yes. Isn't she awful?" young Lechmere candidly ejaculated.

His instructor demurred.

"She's formidable, if you mean that, and it's right she should be; because somehow in her very person, good maiden lady as she is, she represents the might, she represents the traditions and the exploits of the British army. She represents the expansive property of the English name. I think his family can be trusted to come down on him, but every influence should be set in motion. I want to know what yours is. Can *you* do anything in the matter?"

"I can try a couple of rounds with him," said young Lechmere reflectively. "But he knows a fearful lot. He has the most extraordinary ideas."

"Then he has told you some of them—he has taken you into his confidence?"

"I've heard him jaw by the yard," smiled the honest youth. "He has told me he despises it."

"What *is* it he despises? I can't make out."

The most consecutive of Mr. Coyle's nurslings considered a moment, as if he were conscious of a responsibility.

"Why, I think, military glory. He says we take the wrong view of it."

"He oughtn't to talk to *you* that way. It's corrupting the youth of Athens. It's sowing sedition."

"Oh, I'm all right!" said young Lechmere. "And he never told me he meant to chuck it. I always thought he meant to see it through, simply because he had to. He'll argue on any side you like. It's a tremendous pity—I'm sure he'd have a big career."

"Tell him so, then; plead with him; struggle with him—for God's sake."

"I'll do what I can—I'll tell him it's a regular shame."

"Yes, strike *that* note—insist on the disgrace of it."

The young man gave Mr. Coyle a more perceptive glance. "I'm sure he wouldn't do anything dishonourable."

"Well—it won't look right. He must be made to feel *that*—work it up. Give him a comrade's point of view—that of a brother-in-arms."

"That's what I thought we were going to be!" young Lechmere mused romantically, much uplifted by the nature of the mission imposed on him. "He's an awfully good sort."

"No one will think so if he backs out!" said Spencer Coyle.

"They mustn't say it to *me*!" his pupil rejoined with a flush.

Mr. Coyle hesitated a moment, noting his tone and aware that in the perversity of things, though this young man was a born soldier, no excitement would ever attach to *his* alternatives save perhaps on the part of the nice girl to whom at an early day he was sure to be placidly united. "Do you like him very much—do you believe in him?"

Young Lechmere's life in these days was spent in answering terrible questions; but he had never been subjected to so queer an interrogation as this. "Believe in him? Rather!"

"Then *save* him!"

The poor boy was puzzled, as if it were forced upon him by this intensity that there was more in such an appeal than could appear on the surface; and he doubtless felt that he was only entering into a complex situation when after another moment, with his hands in his pockets, he replied hopefully but not pompously: "I daresay I can bring him round!"

II

Before seeing young Lechmere Mr. Coyle had determined to telegraph an inquiry to Miss Wingrave. He had prepaid the answer, which, being promptly put into his hand, brought the interview we have just related to a close. He immediately drove off to Baker Street, where the lady had said she awaited him, and five minutes after he got there, as he sat with Owen Wingrave's remarkable aunt, he repeated over several times, in his angry sadness and with the infallibility of his experience: "He's so intelligent—he's so intelligent!" He had declared it had been a luxury to put such a fellow through.

"Of course he's intelligent, what else could he be? We've never, that I know of, had but *one* idiot in the family!" said Jane Wingrave. This was an allusion that Mr. Coyle could understand, and it brought home to him another of the reasons for the disappointment, the humiliation as it were, of the good people at Paramore, at the same that it gave an example of the conscientious coarseness he had on former occasions observed in his interlocutress. Poor Philip Wingrave, her late brother's eldest son, was literally imbecile and banished from view; deformed, unsocial, irretrievable, he had been relegated to a private asylum and had become among the friends of the family only a little hushed lugubrious legend. All the hopes of the house, picturesque Paramore, now unintermittently old Sir Philip's rather melancholy home (his infirmities would keep him there to the last) were therefore collected on the second boy's head, which nature, as if in compunction for her previous botch, had, in addition to making it strikingly handsome, filled with marked originalities and talents. These two had been the only children of the old man's only son, who, like so many of his ancestors, had given up a gallant young life to the service of his country. Owen Wingrave the elder had received his death-cut, in close-quarters, from an Afghan sabre; the blow had come crashing across his skull. His wife, at that time in India, was about to give birth to her third child; and when the event took place, in darkness and anguish, the baby came lifeless into the world and the mother sank under the multiplication of her woes. The second of the little boys in England, who was at Paramore with his grandfather, became the peculiar charge of his aunt, the only unmarried one, and during the interesting Sunday that, by urgent invitation, Spencer Coyle, busy as he was, had, after consenting to put Owen through, spent under that roof, the celebrated crammer received a vivid impression of the influence exerted at least in intention by Miss Wingrave. Indeed the picture of this short visit remained with the observant little man a curious one—

the vision of an impoverished Jacobean house, shabby and remarkably "creepy," but full of character still and full of felicity as a setting for the distinguished figure of the peaceful old soldier. Sir Philip Wingrave, a relic rather than a celebrity, was a small brown, erect octogenarian, with smouldering eyes and a studied courtesy. He liked to do the diminished honours of his house, but even when with a shaky hand he lighted a bedroom candle for a deprecating guest it was impossible not to feel that beneath the surface he was a merciless old warrior. The eye of the imagination could glance back into his crowded Eastern past—back at episodes in which his scrupulous forms would only have made him more terrible.

Mr. Coyle remembered also two other figures—a faded inoffensive Mrs. Julian, domesticated there by a system of frequent visits as the widow of an officer and a particular friend of Miss Wingrave, and a remarkably clever little girl of eighteen, who was this lady's daughter and who struck the speculative visitor as already formed for other relations. She was very impertinent to Owen, and in the course of a long walk that he had taken with the young man and the effect of which, in much talk, had been to clinch his high opinion of him, he had learned (for Owen chattered confidentially) that Mrs. Julian was the sister of a very gallant gentleman, Captain Hume-Walker, of the Artillery, who had fallen in the Indian Mutiny and between whom and Miss Wingrave (it had been that lady's one known concession) a passage of some delicacy, taking a tragic turn, was believed to have been enacted. They had been engaged to be married, but she had given way to the jealousy of her nature—had broken with him and sent him off to his fate, which had been horrible. A passionate sense of having wronged him, a hard eternal remorse had thereupon taken possession of her, and when his poor sister, linked also to a soldier, had by a still heavier blow been left almost without resources, she had devoted herself charitably to a long expiation. She had sought comfort in taking Mrs. Julian to live much of the time at Paramore, where she became an unremunerated though not uncriticised housekeeper, and Spencer Coyle suspected that it was a part of this comfort that she could at her leisure trample on her. The impression of Jane Wingrave was not the faintest he had gathered on that intensifying Sunday—an occasion singularly tinged for him with the sense of bereavement and mourning and memory, of names never mentioned, of the far-away plaint of widows and the echoes of battles and bad news. It was all military indeed, and Mr. Coyle was made to shudder a little at the profession of which he helped to open the door to harmless young men. Miss Wingrave moreover might have made such a bad conscience worse— so cold and clear a good one looked at him out of her hard, fine eyes and trumpeted in her sonorous voice.

She was a high, distinguished person; angular but not awkward, with a large forehead and abundant black hair, arranged like that of a woman conceiving perhaps excusably of her head as "noble," and irregularly streaked to-day with white. If however she represented for Spencer Coyle the genius of a military race it was not that she had the step of a grenadier or the vocabulary of a camp-follower; it was only that such sympathies were vividly implied in the general fact to which her very presence and each of her actions and glances and tones were a constant and direct allusion—the paramount valour of her family. If she was military it was because she sprang from a military house and because she wouldn't for the world have been anything but what the Wingraves had been. She was almost vulgar about her ancestors, and if one had been tempted to quarrel with her one would have found a fair pretext in her defective sense of proportion. This temptation however said nothing to Spencer Coyle, for whom as a strong character revealing itself in colour and sound she was a spectacle and who was glad to regard her as a force exerted on his own side. He wished her nephew had more of her narrowness instead of being almost cursed with the tendency to look at things in their relations. He wondered why when she came up to town she always resorted to Baker Street for lodgings. He had never known nor heard of Baker Street as a residence—he associated it only with bazaars and photographers. He divined in her a rigid indifference to everything that was not the passion of her life. Nothing really mattered to her but that, and she would have occupied apartments in Whitechapel if they had been a feature in her tactics. She had received her visitor in a large cold, faded room, furnished with slippery seats and decorated with alabaster vases and wax-flowers. The only little personal comfort for which she appeared to have looked out was a fat catalogue of the Army and Navy Stores, which reposed on a vast, desolate table-cover of false blue. Her clear forehead—it was like a porcelain slate, a receptacle for addresses and sums—had flushed when her nephew's crammer told her the extraordinary news; but he saw she was fortunately more angry than frightened. She had essentially, she would always have, too little imagination for fear, and the healthy habit moreover of facing everything had taught her that the occasion usually found her a quantity to reckon with. Mr. Coyle saw that her only fear at present could have been that of not being able to prevent her nephew from being absurd and that to such an apprehension as this she was in fact inaccessible. Practically too she was not troubled by surprise; she recognised none of the futile, none of the subtle sentiments. If Philip had for an hour made a fool of himself she was angry; disconcerted as she would have been on learning that he had confessed to debts or fallen in love with a low girl. But there remained in any annoyance the saving fact that no one could make a fool of *her*.

"I don't know when I've taken such an interest in a young man—I think I never have, since I began to handle them," Mr. Coyle said. "I like him, I believe in him—it's been a delight to see how he was going."

"Oh, I know how they go!" Miss Wingrave threw back her head with a familiar briskness, as if a rapid procession of the generations had flashed before her, rattling their scabbards and spurs. Spencer Coyle recognised the intimation that she had nothing to learn from anybody about the natural carriage of a Wingrave, and he even felt convicted by her next words of being, in her eyes, with the troubled story of his check, his weak complaint of his pupil, rather a poor creature. "If you like him," she exclaimed, "for mercy's sake keep him quiet!"

Mr. Coyle began to explain to her that this was less easy than she appeared to imagine; but he perceived that she understood very little of what he said. The more he insisted that the boy had a kind of intellectual independence, the more this struck her as a conclusive proof that her nephew was a Wingrave and a soldier. It was not till he mentioned to her that Owen had spoken of the profession of arms as of something that would be "beneath" him, it was not till her attention was arrested by this intenser light on the complexity of the problem that Miss Wingrave broke out after a moment's stupefied reflection: "Send him to see me immediately!"

"That's exactly what I wanted to ask your leave to do. But I've wanted also to prepare you for the worst, to make you understand that he strikes me as really obstinate and to suggest to you that the most powerful arguments at your command—especially if you should be able to put your hand on some intensely practical one—will be none too effective."

"I think I've got a powerful argument." Miss Wingrave looked very hard at her visitor. He didn't know in the least what it was, but he begged her to put it forward without delay. He promised that their young man should come to Baker Street that evening, mentioning however that he had already urged him to spend without delay a couple of days at Eastbourne. This led Jane Wingrave to inquire with surprise what virtue there might be in *that* expensive remedy, and to reply with decision when Mr. Coyle had said "The virtue of a little rest, a little change, a little relief to overwrought nerves," "Ah, don't coddle him—he's costing us a great deal of money! I'll talk to him and I'll take him down to Paramore; then I'll send him back to you straightened out."

Spencer Coyle hailed this pledge superficially with satisfaction, but before he quitted Miss Wingrave he became conscious that he had really taken on a new anxiety—a restlessness that made him say to himself, groaning inwardly: "Oh, she is a grenadier at bottom, and she'll have no tact. I don't know what her powerful argument is; I'm only afraid she'll be stupid and make him worse. The old man's better—*he's* capable of tact, though he's not quite an extinct volcano. Owen will probably put him in a rage. In short the difficulty is that the boy's the best of them."

Spencer Coyle felt afresh that evening at dinner that the boy was the best of them. Young Wingrave (who, he was pleased to observe, had not yet proceeded to the seaside) appeared at the repast as usual, looking inevitably a little self-conscious, but not too original for Bayswater. He talked very naturally to Mrs. Coyle, who had thought him from the first the most beautiful young man they had ever received; so that the person most ill at ease was poor Lechmere, who took great trouble, as if from the deepest delicacy, not to meet the eye of his misguided mate. Spencer Coyle however paid the penalty of his own profundity in feeling more and more worried; he could so easily see that there were all sorts of things in his young friend that the people of Paramore wouldn't understand. He began even already to react against the notion of his being harassed—to reflect that after all he had a right to his ideas—to remember that he was of a substance too fine to be in fairness roughly used. It was in this way that the ardent little crammer, with his whimsical perceptions and complicated sympathies, was generally condemned not to settle down comfortably either into his displeasures or into his enthusiasms. His love of the real truth never gave him a chance to enjoy them. He mentioned to Wingrave after dinner the propriety of an immediate visit to Baker Street, and the young man, looking "queer," as he thought—that is smiling again with the exaggerated glory he had shown in their recent interview—went off to face the ordeal. Spencer Coyle noted that he was scared—he was afraid of his aunt; but somehow this didn't strike him as a sign of pusillanimity. *He* should have been scared, he was well aware, in the poor boy's place, and the sight of his pupil marching up to the battery in spite of his terrors was a positive suggestion of the temperament of the soldier. Many a plucky youth would have shirked this particular peril.

"He *has* got ideas!" young Lechmere broke out to his instructor after his comrade had quitted the house. He was evidently bewildered and agitated—he had an emotion to work off. He had before dinner gone straight at his friend, as Mr. Coyle had requested, and had elicited from him that his scruples were founded on an overwhelming conviction of the stupidity—the "crass barbarism" he called it—of war. His great complaint was that people hadn't invented anything cleverer, and he was determined to show, the only way he could, that *he* wasn't such an ass.

"And he thinks all the great generals ought to have been shot, and that Napoleon Bonaparte in particular, the greatest, was a criminal, a monster for whom language has no adequate name!" Mr. Coyle rejoined, completing young Lechmere's picture. "He favoured you, I see, with exactly the same pearls of wisdom that he produced for me. But I want to know what *you* said."

"I said they were awful rot!" Young Lechmere spoke with emphasis, and he was slightly surprised to hear Mr. Coyle laugh incongruously at this just declaration and then after a moment continue:

"It's all very curious—I daresay there's something in it. But it's a pity!"

"He told me when it was that the question began to strike him in that light. Four or five years ago, when he did a lot of reading about all the great swells and their campaigns—Hannibal and Julius Cæsar, Marlborough and Frederick and Bonaparte. He *has* done a lot of reading, and he says it opened his eyes. He says that a wave of disgust rolled over him. He talked about the 'immeasurable misery' of wars, and asked me why nations don't tear to pieces the governments, the rulers that go in for them. He hates poor old Bonaparte worst of all."

"Well, poor old Bonaparte was a brute. He was a frightful ruffian," Mr. Coyle unexpectedly declared. "But I suppose you didn't admit that."

"Oh, I daresay he was objectionable, and I'm very glad we laid him on his back. But the point I made to Wingrave was that his own behaviour would excite no end of remark." Young Lechmere hesitated an instant, then he added: "I told him he must be prepared for the worst."

"Of course he asked you what you meant by the 'worst,'" said Spencer Coyle.

"Yes, he asked me that, and do you know what I said? I said people would say that his conscientious scruples and his wave of disgust are only a pretext. Then he asked 'A pretext for what?'"

"Ah, he rather had you there!" Mr. Coyle exclaimed with a little laugh that was mystifying to his pupil.

"Not a bit—for I told him."

"What did you tell him?"

Once more, for a few seconds, with his conscious eyes in his instructor's, the young man hung fire.

"Why, what we spoke of a few hours ago. The appearance he'd present of not having——" The honest youth faltered a moment, then brought it out: "The military temperament, don't you know? But do you know what he said to that?" young Lechmere went on.

"Damn the military temperament!" the crammer promptly replied.

Young Lechmere stared. Mr. Coyle's tone left him uncertain if he were attributing the phrase to Wingrave or uttering his own opinion, but he exclaimed:

"Those were exactly his words!"

"He doesn't care," said Mr. Coyle.

"Perhaps not. But it isn't fair for him to abuse us fellows. I told him it's the finest temperament in the world, and that there's nothing so splendid as pluck and heroism."

"Ah! there you had *him*."

"I told him it was unworthy of him to abuse a gallant, a magnificent profession. I told him there's no type so fine as that of the soldier doing his duty."

"That's essentially *your* type, my dear boy." Young Lechmere blushed; he couldn't make out (and the danger was naturally unexpected to him) whether at that moment he didn't exist mainly for the recreation of his friend. But he was partly reassured by the genial way this friend continued, laying a hand on his shoulder: "Keep *at* him that way! we may do something. I'm extremely obliged to you." Another doubt however remained unassuaged—a doubt which led him to exclaim to Mr. Coyle before they dropped the painful subject:

"He *doesn't* care! But it's awfully odd he shouldn't!"

"So it is, but remember what you said this afternoon—I mean about your not advising people to make insinuations to *you*."

"I believe I should knock a fellow down!" said young Lechmere. Mr. Coyle had got up; the conversation had taken place while they sat together after Mrs. Coyle's withdrawal from the dinner-table and the head of the establishment administered to his disciple, on principles that were a part of his thoroughness, a glass of excellent claret. The disciple, also on his feet, lingered an instant, not for another "go," as he would have called it, at the decanter, but to wipe his microscopic moustache with prolonged and unusual care. His companion saw he had something to bring out which required a final effort, and waited for him an instant with a hand on the knob of the door. Then as young Lechmere approached him Spencer Coyle grew conscious of an unwonted intensity in the round and ingenuous face. The boy was nervous, but he tried to behave like a man of the world. "Of course, it's between ourselves," he stammered, "and I wouldn't breathe such a word to any one who wasn't interested in poor Wingrave as you are. But do you think he funks it?"

Mr. Coyle looked at him so hard for an instant that he was visibly frightened at what he had said.

"Funks it! Funks what?"

"Why, what we're talking about—the service." Young Lechmere gave a little gulp and added with a *naïveté* almost pathetic to Spencer Coyle: "The dangers, you know!"

"Do you mean he's thinking of his skin?"

Young Lechmere's eyes expanded appealingly, and what his instructor saw in his pink face—he even thought he saw a tear—was the dread of a disappointment shocking in the degree in which the loyalty of admiration had been great.

"Is he—is he *afraid?*" repeated the honest lad, with a quaver of suspense.

"Dear no!" said Spencer Coyle, turning his back.

Young Lechmere felt a little snubbed and even a little ashamed; but he felt still more relieved.

III

Less than a week after this Spencer Coyle received a note from Miss Wingrave, who had immediately quitted London with her nephew. She proposed that he should come down to Paramore for the following Sunday—Owen was really so tiresome. On the spot, in that house of examples and memories and in combination with her poor dear father, who was "dreadfully annoyed," it might be worth their while to make a last stand. Mr. Coyle read between the lines of this letter that the party at Paramore had got over a good deal of ground since Miss Wingrave, in Baker Street, had treated his despair as superficial. She was not an insinuating woman, but she went so far as to put the question on the ground of his conferring a particular favour on an afflicted family; and she expressed the pleasure it would give them if he should be accompanied by Mrs. Coyle, for whom she inclosed a separate invitation. She mentioned that she was also writing, subject to Mr. Coyle's approval, to young Lechmere. She thought such a nice manly boy might do her wretched nephew some good. The celebrated crammer determined to embrace this opportunity; and now it was the case not so much that he was angry as that he was anxious. As he directed his answer to Miss Wingrave's letter he caught himself smiling at the thought that at bottom he was going to defend his young friend rather than to attack him. He said to his wife, who was a fair, fresh, slow woman—a person of much more presence than himself—that she had better take Miss Wingrave at her word: it was such an extraordinary, such a fascinating specimen of an old English home. This last allusion was amicably sarcastic—he had already accused the good lady more than once of being in love with Owen Wingrave. She admitted that she was, she even gloried in her passion; which shows that the subject, between them, was treated in a liberal spirit. She carried out the joke by accepting the invitation with eagerness. Young Lechmere was delighted to do the same; his instructor had good-naturedly taken the view that the little break would freshen him up for his last spurt.

It was the fact that the occupants of Paramore did indeed take their trouble hard that struck Spencer Coyle after he had been an hour or two in that fine old house. This very short second visit, beginning on the Saturday evening, was to constitute the strangest episode of his life. As soon as he found himself in private with his wife—they had retired to dress for dinner—they called each other's attention with effusion and almost with alarm to the sinister gloom that was stamped on the place. The house was admirable with its old grey front which came forward in wings so as to form three sides of a square, but Mrs. Coyle made no scruple to declare that if she had known in advance the sort of impression she was going to receive she would never have put her foot in it. She characterized it as "uncanny," she accused her husband of not having warned her properly. He had mentioned to her in advance certain facts, but while she almost feverishly dressed she had innumerable questions to ask. He hadn't told her about the girl, the extraordinary girl, Miss Julian—that is, he hadn't told her that this young lady, who in plain terms was a mere dependent, would be in effect, and as a consequence of the way she carried herself, the most important person in the house. Mrs. Coyle was already prepared to announce that she hated Miss Julian's affectations. Her husband above all hadn't told her that they should find their young charge looking five years older.

"I couldn't imagine that," said Mr. Coyle, "nor that the character of the crisis here would be quite so perceptible. But I suggested to Miss Wingrave the other day that they should press her nephew in real earnest, and she has taken me at my word. They've cut off his supplies—they're trying to starve him out. That's not what I meant—but indeed I don't quite *know* to-day what I meant. Owen feels the pressure, but he won't yield." The strange thing was that, now that he was there, the versatile little coach felt still more that his own spirit had been caught up by a wave of reaction. If he was there it was because he was on poor Owen's side. His whole impression, his whole apprehension, had on the spot become much deeper. There was something in the dear boy's very resistance that began to charm him. When his wife, in the intimacy of the conference I have mentioned, threw off the mask and commended even with extravagance the stand his pupil had taken (he was too good to be a horrid soldier and it was noble of him to suffer for his convictions—wasn't he as upright as a young hero, even though as pale as a Christian martyr?) the good lady only expressed the sympathy which, under cover of regarding his young friend as a rare exception, he had already recognised in his own soul.

For, half an hour ago, after they had had superficial tea in the brown old hall of the house, his young friend had proposed to him, before going to dress, to take a turn outside, and had even, on the terrace, as they walked together to one of the far ends of it, passed his hand entreatingly into his companion's arm, permitting himself thus a familiarity unusual between pupil and master and calculated to show that he had guessed whom he could most depend on to be kind to him. Spencer Coyle on his own side had guessed something, so that he was not surprised at the boy's having a particular confidence to make. He had felt on arriving that each member of the party had wished to get hold of him first, and he knew that at that moment Jane Wingrave was peering through the ancient blur of one of the windows (the house had been modernised so little that the thick dim panes were three centuries old) to see if her nephew looked as if he were poisoning the visitor's mind. Mr. Coyle lost no time therefore in reminding the youth (and he took care to laugh as he did so) that he had not come down to Paramore to be corrupted. He had come down to make, face to face, a last appeal to him—he hoped it wouldn't be utterly vain. Owen smiled sadly as they went, asking him if he thought he had the general air of a fellow who was going to knock under.

"I think you look strange—I think you look ill," Spencer Coyle said very honestly. They had paused at the end of the terrace.

"I've had to exercise a great power of resistance, and it rather takes it out of one."

"Ah, my dear boy, I wish your great power—for you evidently possess it—were exerted in a better cause!"

Owen Wingrave smiled down at his small instructor. "I don't believe that!" Then he added, to explain why: "Isn't what you want, if you're so good as to think well of my character, to see me exert *most* power, in whatever direction? Well, *this* is the way I exert most." Owen Wingrave went on to relate that he had had some terrible hours with his grandfather, who had denounced him in a way to make one's hair stand up on one's head. He had expected them not to like it, not a bit, but he had had no idea they would make such a row. His aunt was different, but she was equally insulting. Oh, they had made him feel they were ashamed of him; they accused him of putting a public dishonour on their name. He was the only one who had ever backed out—he was the first for three hundred years. Every one had known he was to go up, and now every one would know he was a young hypocrite who suddenly pretended to have scruples. They talked of his scruples as you wouldn't talk of a cannibal's god. His grandfather had called him outrageous names. "He called me—he called me——" Here the young man faltered, his voice failed him. He looked as haggard as was possible to a young man in such magnificent health.

"I probably know!" said Spencer Coyle, with a nervous laugh.

Owen Wingrave's clouded eyes, as if they were following the far-off consequences of things, rested for an instant on a distant object. Then they met his companion's and for another moment sounded them deeply. "It isn't true. No, it isn't. It's not *that*!"

"I don't suppose it is! But what *do* you propose instead of it?"

"Instead of what?"

"Instead of the stupid solution of war. If you take that away you should suggest at least a substitute."

"That's for the people in charge, for governments and cabinets," said Owen Wingrave. "*They*'ll arrive soon enough at a substitute, in the particular case, if they're made to understand that they'll be hung if they don't find one. Make it a capital crime—that'll quicken the wits of ministers!" His eyes brightened as he spoke, and he looked assured and exalted. Mr. Coyle gave a sigh of perplexed resignation—it was a monomania. He fancied after this for a moment that Owen was going to ask him if he too thought he was a coward; but he was relieved to observe that he either didn't suspect him of it or shrank uncomfortably from putting the question to the test. Spencer Coyle wished to show confidence, but somehow a direct assurance that he didn't doubt of his courage appeared too gross a compliment—it would be like saying he didn't doubt of his honesty. The difficulty was presently averted by Owen's continuing: "My grandfather can't break the entail, but I shall have nothing but this place, which, as you know, is small and, with the way rents are going, has quite ceased to yield an income. He has some money—not much, but such as it is he cuts me off. My aunt does the same—she has let me know her intentions. She was to have left me her six hundred a year. It was all settled; but now what's settled is that I don't get a penny of it if I give up the army. I must add in fairness that I have from my mother three hundred a year of my own. And I tell you the simple truth when I say that I don't care a rap for the loss of the money." The young man drew a long, slow breath, like a creature in pain; then he subjoined: "*That's* not what worries me!"

"What are you going to do?" asked Spencer Coyle.

"I don't know; perhaps nothing. Nothing great, at all events. Only something peaceful!"

Owen gave a weary smile, as if, worried as he was, he could yet appreciate the humorous effect of such a declaration from a Wingrave; but what it suggested to his companion, who looked up at him with a sense that he was after all not a Wingrave for nothing and had a military steadiness under fire, was the exasperation that such a programme, uttered in such a way and striking them as the last word of the inglorious, might well have engendered on the part of his grandfather and his aunt. "Perhaps nothing"—when he might carry on the great tradition! Yes, he wasn't weak, and he was interesting; but there *was* a point of view from which he was provoking. "What *is* it then that worries you?" Mr. Coyle demanded.

"Oh, the house—the very air and feeling of it. There are strange voices in it that seem to mutter at me—to say dreadful things as I pass. I mean the general consciousness and responsibility of what I'm doing. Of course it hasn't been easy for me—not a bit. I assure you I don't enjoy it." With a light in them that was like a longing for justice Owen again bent his eyes on those of the little coach; then he pursued: "I've started up all the old ghosts. The very portraits glower at me on the walls. There's one of my great-great-grandfather (the one the extraordinary story you know is about—the old fellow who hangs on the second landing of the big staircase) that fairly stirs on the canvas—just heaves a little—when I come near it. I have to go up and down stairs—it's rather awkward! It's what my aunt calls the family circle. It's all constituted here, it's a kind of indestructible presence, it stretches away into the past, and when I came back with her the other day Miss Wingrave told me I wouldn't have the impudence to stand in the midst of it and say such things. I had to say them to my grandfather; but now that I've said them it seems to me that the question's ended. I want to go away—I don't care if I never come back again."

"Oh, you *are* a soldier; you must fight it out!" Mr. Coyle laughed.

The young man seemed discouraged at his levity, but as they turned round, strolling back in the direction from which they had come, he himself smiled faintly after an instant and replied:

"Ah, we're tainted—all!"

They walked in silence part of the way to the old portico; then Spencer Coyle, stopping short after having assured himself that he was at a sufficient distance from the house not to be heard, suddenly put the question: "What does Miss Julian say?"

"Miss Julian?" Owen had perceptibly coloured.

"I'm sure *she* hasn't concealed her opinion."

"Oh, it's the opinion of the family circle, for she's a member of it of course. And then she has her own as well."

"Her own opinion?"

"Her own family circle."

"Do you mean her mother—that patient lady?"

"I mean more particularly her father, who fell in battle. And her grandfather, and *his* father, and her uncles and great-uncles—they all fell in battle."

"Hasn't the sacrifice of so many lives been sufficient? Why should she sacrifice you?"

"Oh, she *hates* me!" Owen declared, as they resumed their walk.

"Ah, the hatred of pretty girls for fine young men!" exclaimed Spencer Coyle.

He didn't believe in it, but his wife did, it appeared perfectly, when he mentioned this conversation while, in the fashion that has been described, the visitors dressed for dinner. Mrs. Coyle had already discovered that nothing could have been nastier than Miss Julian's manner to the disgraced youth during the half-hour the party had spent in the hall; and it was this lady's judgment that one must have had no eyes in one's head not to see that she was already trying outrageously to flirt with young Lechmere. It was a pity they had brought that silly boy: he was down in the hall with her at that moment. Spencer Coyle's version was different; he thought there were finer elements involved. The girl's footing in the house was inexplicable on any ground save that of her being predestined to Miss Wingrave's nephew. As the niece of Miss Wingrave's own unhappy intended she had been dedicated early by this lady to the office of healing by a union with Owen the tragic breach that had separated their elders; and if in reply to this it was to be said that a girl of spirit couldn't enjoy in such a matter having her duty cut out for her, Owen's enlightened friend was ready with the argument that a young person in Miss Julian's position would never be such a fool as really to quarrel with a capital chance. She was familiar at Paramore and she felt safe; therefore she might trust herself to the amusement of pretending that she had her option. But it was all innocent coquetry. She had a curious charm, and it was vain to pretend that the heir of that house wouldn't seem good enough to a girl, clever as she might be, of eighteen. Mrs. Coyle reminded her husband that the poor young man was precisely now *not* of that house: this problem was among the questions that exercised their wits after the two men had taken the turn on the terrace. Spencer Coyle told his wife that Owen was afraid of the portrait of his great-great-grandfather. He would show it to her, since she hadn't noticed it, on their way down stairs.

"Why of his great-great-grandfather more than of any of the others?"

"Oh, because he's the most formidable. He's the one who's sometimes seen."

"Seen where?" Mrs. Coyle had turned round with a jerk.

"In the room he was found dead in—the White Room they've always called it."

"Do you mean to say the house has a *ghost?*" Mrs. Coyle almost shrieked. "You brought me here without telling me?"

"Didn't I mention it after my other visit?"

"Not a word. You only talked about Miss Wingrave."

"Oh, I was full of the story—you have simply forgotten."

"Then you should have reminded me!"

"If I had thought of it I would have held my peace, for you wouldn't have come."

"I wish, indeed, I hadn't!" cried Mrs. Coyle. "What *is* the story?"

"Oh, a deed of violence that took place here ages ago. I think it was in George the First's time. Colonel Wingrave, one of their ancestors, struck in a fit of passion one of his children, a lad just growing up, a blow on the head of which the unhappy child died. The matter was hushed up for the hour—some other explanation was put about. The poor boy was laid out in one of those rooms on the other side of the house, and amid strange smothered rumours the funeral was hurried on. The next morning, when the household assembled, Colonel Wingrave was missing; he was looked for vainly, and at last it occurred to some one that he might perhaps be in the room from which his child had been carried to burial. The seeker knocked without an answer—then opened the door. Colonel Wingrave lay dead on the floor, in his clothes, as if he had reeled and fallen back, without a wound, without a mark, without anything in his appearance to indicate that he had either struggled or suffered. He was a strong, sound man—there was nothing to account for such a catastrophe. He is supposed to have gone to the room during the night, just before going to bed, in some fit of compunction or some fascination of dread. It was only after this that the truth about the boy came out. But no one ever sleeps in the room."

Mrs. Coyle had fairly turned pale. "I hope not! Thank heaven they haven't put *us* there!"

"We're at a comfortable distance; but I've seen the gruesome chamber."

"Do you mean you've been *in* it?"

"For a few moments. They're rather proud of it and my young friend showed it to me when I was here before."

Mrs. Coyle stared. "And what is it like?"

"Simply like an empty, dull, old-fashioned bedroom, rather big, with the things of the 'period' in it. It's panelled from floor to ceiling, and the panels evidently, years and years ago, were painted white. But the paint has darkened with time and there are three or four quaint little ancient 'samplers,' framed and glazed, hung on the walls."

Mrs. Coyle looked round with a shudder. "I'm glad there are no samplers here! I never heard anything so jumpy! Come down to dinner."

On the staircase as they went down her husband showed her the portrait of Colonel Wingrave—rather a vigorous representation, for the place and period, of a gentleman with a hard, handsome face, in a red coat and a peruke. Mrs. Coyle declared that his descendant Sir Philip was wonderfully like him; and her husband could fancy, though he kept it to himself, that if one should have the courage to walk about the old corridors of Paramore at night one might meet a figure that resembled him roaming, with the restlessness of a ghost, hand in hand with the figure of a tall boy. As he proceeded to the drawing-room with his wife he found himself suddenly wishing that he had made more of a point of his pupil's going to Eastbourne. The evening however seemed to have taken upon itself to dissipate any such whimsical forebodings, for the grimness of the family circle, as Spencer Coyle had preconceived its composition, was mitigated by an infusion of the "neighbourhood." The company at dinner was recruited by two cheerful couples—one of them the vicar and his wife, and by a silent young man who had come down to fish. This was a relief to Mr. Coyle, who had begun to wonder what was after all expected of him and why he had been such a fool as to come, and who now felt that for the first hours at least the situation would not have directly to be dealt with. Indeed he found, as he had found before, sufficient occupation for his ingenuity in reading the various symptoms of which the picture before him was an expression. He should probably have an irritating day on the morrow: he foresaw the difficulty of the long decorous Sunday and how dry Jane Wingrave's ideas, elicited in a strenuous conference, would taste. She and her father would make him feel that they depended upon him for the impossible, and if they should try to associate him with a merely stupid policy he might end by telling them what he thought of it—an accident not required to make his visit a sensible mistake. The old man's actual design was evidently to let their friends see in it a positive mark of their being all right. The presence of the great London coach was tantamount to a profession of faith in the results of the impending examination. It had clearly been obtained from Owen, rather to Spencer Coyle's surprise, that he would do nothing to interfere with the apparent harmony. He let the allusions to his hard work pass and, holding his tongue about his affairs, talked to the ladies as amicably as if he had not been "cut off." When Spencer Coyle looked at him once or twice across the table, catching his eye, which showed an indefinable passion, he saw a puzzling pathos in his laughing face: one couldn't resist a pang for a young lamb so visibly marked for sacrifice. "Hang him—what a pity he's such a fighter!" he privately sighed, with a want of logic that was only superficial.

This idea however would have absorbed him more if so much of his attention had not been given to Kate Julian, who now that he had her well before him struck him as a remarkable and even as a possibly fascinating young woman. The fascination resided not in any extraordinary prettiness, for if she was handsome, with her long Eastern eyes, her magnificent hair and her general unabashed originality, he had seen complexions rosier and features that pleased him more: it resided in a strange impression that she gave of being exactly the sort of person whom, in her position, common considerations, those of prudence and perhaps even a little those of decorum, would have enjoined on her not to be. She was what was vulgarly termed a dependant—penniless, patronized, tolerated; but something in her aspect and manner signified that if her situation was inferior, her spirit, to make up for it, was above precautions or submissions. It was not in the least that she was aggressive, she was too indifferent for that; it was only as if, having nothing either to gain or to lose, she could afford to do as she liked. It occurred to Spencer Coyle that she might really have had more at stake than her imagination appeared to take account of; whatever it was at any rate he had never seen a young woman at less pains to be on the safe side. He wondered inevitably how the peace was kept between Jane Wingrave and such an inmate as this; but those questions of course were unfathomable deeps. Perhaps Kate Julian lorded it even over her protectress. The other time he was at Paramore he had received an impression that, with Sir Philip beside her, the girl could fight with her back to the wall. She amused Sir Philip, she charmed him, and he liked people who weren't afraid; between him and his daughter moreover there was no doubt which was the higher in command. Miss Wingrave took many things for granted, and most of all the rigour of discipline and the fate of the vanquished and the captive.

But between their clever boy and so original a companion of his childhood what odd relation would have grown up? It couldn't be indifference, and yet on the part of happy, handsome, youthful creatures it was still less likely to be aversion. They weren't Paul and Virginia, but they must have had their common summer and their idyll: no nice girl could have disliked such a nice fellow for anything but not liking *her*, and no nice fellow could have resisted such propinquity. Mr. Coyle remembered indeed that Mrs. Julian had spoken to him as if the propinquity had been by no means constant, owing to her daughter's absences at school, to say nothing of Owen's; her visits to a few friends who were so kind as to "take her" from time to time; her sojourns in London—so difficult to manage, but still managed by God's help—for "advantages," for drawing and singing, especially drawing or rather painting, in oils, in which she had had immense success. But the good lady had also mentioned that the young people were quite brother and sister, which *was* a little, after all, like Paul and Virginia. Mrs. Coyle had been right, and it was apparent that Virginia was doing her best to make the time pass agreeably for young Lechmere. There was no such whirl of conversation as to render it an effort for Mr. Coyle to reflect on these things, for the tone of the occasion, thanks principally to the other guests, was not disposed to stray—it tended to the repetition of anecdote and the discussion of rents, topics that huddled together like uneasy animals. He could judge how intensely his hosts wished the evening to pass off as if nothing had happened; and this gave him the measure of their private resentment. Before dinner was over he found himself fidgetty about his second pupil. Young Lechmere, since he began to cram, had done all that might have been expected of him; but this couldn't blind his instructor to a present perception of his being in moments of relaxation as innocent as a babe. Mr. Coyle had considered that the amusements of Paramore would probably give him a fillip, and the poor fellow's manner testified to the soundness of the forecast. The fillip had been unmistakably administered; it had come in the form of a revelation. The light on young Lechmere's brow announced with a candour that was almost an appeal for compassion, or at least a deprecation of ridicule, that he had never seen anything like Miss Julian.

IV

In the drawing-room after dinner the girl found an occasion to approach Spencer Coyle. She stood before him a moment, smiling while she opened and shut her fan, and then she said abruptly, raising her strange eyes: "I know what you've come for, but it isn't any use."

"I've come to look after *you* a little. Isn't *that* any use?"

"It's very kind. But I'm not the question of the hour. You won't do anything with Owen."

Spencer Coyle hesitated a moment. "What will *you* do with his young friend?"

She stared, looked round her.

"Mr. Lechmere? Oh, poor little lad! We've been talking about Owen. He admires him so."

"So do I. I should tell you that."

"So do we all. That's why we're in such despair."

"Personally then you'd *like* him to be a soldier?" Spencer Coyle inquired.

"I've quite set my heart on it. I adore the army and I'm awfully fond of my old playmate," said Miss Julian.

Her interlocutor remembered the young man's own different version of her attitude; but he judged it loyal not to challenge the girl.

"It's not conceivable that your old playmate shouldn't be fond of you. He must therefore wish to please you; and I don't see why—between you—you don't set the matter right."

"Wish to please me!" Miss Julian exclaimed. "I'm sorry to say he shows no such desire. He thinks me an impudent wretch. I've told him what I think of *him*, and he simply hates me."

"But you think so highly! You just told me you admire him."

"His talents, his possibilities, yes; even his appearance, if I may allude to such a matter. But I don't admire his present behaviour."

"Have you had the question out with him?" Spencer Coyle asked.

"Oh, yes, I've ventured to be frank—the occasion seemed to excuse it. He couldn't like what I said."

"What did you say?"

Miss Julian, thinking a moment, opened and shut her fan again.

"Why, that such conduct isn't that of a gentleman!"

After she had spoken her eyes met Spencer Coyle's, who looked into their charming depths.

"Do you want then so much to send him off to be killed?"

"How odd for *you* to ask that—in such a way!" she replied with a laugh. "I don't understand your position: I thought your line was to *make* soldiers!"

"You should take my little joke. But, as regards Owen Wingrave, there's no 'making' needed," Mr. Coyle added. "To my sense"—the little crammer paused a moment, as if with a consciousness of responsibility for his paradox—"to my sense he *is*, in a high sense of the term, a fighting man."

"Ah, let him prove it!" the girl exclaimed, turning away.

Spencer Coyle let her go; there was something in her tone that annoyed and even a little shocked him. There had evidently been a violent passage between these young people, and the reflection that such a matter was after all none of his business only made him more sore. It was indeed a military house, and she was at any rate a person who placed her ideal of manhood (young persons doubtless always had their ideals of manhood) in the type of the belted warrior. It was a taste like another; but, even a quarter of an hour later, finding himself near young Lechmere, in whom this type was embodied, Spencer Coyle was still so ruffled that he addressed the innocent lad with a certain magisterial dryness. "You're not to sit up late, you know. That's not what I brought you down for." The dinner-guests were taking leave and the bedroom candles twinkled in a monitory row. Young Lechmere however was too agreeably agitated to be accessible to a snub: he had a happy preoccupation which almost engendered a grin.

"I'm only too eager for bedtime. Do you know there's an awfully jolly room?"

"Surely they haven't put you there?"

"No indeed: no one has passed a night in it for ages. But that's exactly what I want to do—it would be tremendous fun."

"And have you been trying to get Miss Julian's permission?"

"Oh, *she* can't give leave, she says. But she believes in it, and she maintains that no man dare."

"No man *shall*. A man in your critical position in particular must have a quiet night," said Spencer Coyle.

Young Lechmere gave a disappointed but reasonable sigh.

"Oh, all right. But mayn't I sit up for a little go at Wingrave? I haven't had any yet."

Mr. Coyle looked at his watch.

"You may smoke *one* cigarette."

He felt a hand on his shoulder, and he turned round to see his wife tilting candle-grease upon his coat. The ladies were going to bed and it was Sir Philip's inveterate hour; but Mrs. Coyle confided to her husband that after the dreadful things he had told her she positively declined to be left alone, for no matter how short an interval, in any part of the house. He promised to follow her within three minutes, and after the orthodox handshakes the ladies rustled away. The forms were kept up at Paramore as bravely as if the old house had no present heartache. The only one of which Spencer Coyle noticed the omission was some salutation to himself from Kate Julian. She gave him neither a word nor a glance, but he saw her look hard at Owen Wingrave. Her mother, timid and pitying, was apparently the only person from whom this young man caught an inclination of the head. Miss Wingrave marshalled the three ladies—her little procession of twinkling tapers—up the wide oaken stairs and past the watching portrait of her ill-fated ancestor. Sir Philip's servant appeared and offered his arm to the old man, who turned a perpendicular back on poor Owen when the boy made a vague movement to anticipate this office. Spencer Coyle learned afterwards that before Owen had forfeited favour it had always, when he was at home, been his privilege at bedtime to conduct his grandfather ceremoniously to rest. Sir Philip's habits were contemptuously different now. His apartments were on the lower floor and he shuffled stiffly off to them with his valet's help, after fixing for a moment significantly on the most responsible of his visitors the thick red ray, like the glow of stirred embers, that always made his eyes conflict oddly with his mild manners. They seemed to say to Spencer Coyle "We'll let the young scoundrel have it to-morrow!" One might have gathered from them that the young scoundrel, who had now strolled to the other end of the hall, had at least forged a cheque. Mr. Coyle watched him an instant, saw him drop nervously into a chair and then with a restless movement get up. The same movement brought him back to where his late instructor stood addressing a last injunction to young Lechmere.

"I'm going to bed and I should like you particularly to conform to what I said to you a short time ago. Smoke a single cigarette with your friend here and then go to your room. You'll have me down on you if I hear of your having, during the night, tried any preposterous games." Young Lechmere, looking down with his hands in his pockets, said nothing—he only poked at the corner of a rug with his toe; so that Spencer Coyle, dissatisfied with so tacit a pledge, presently went on, to Owen: "I must request you, Wingrave, not to keep this sensitive subject sitting up—and indeed to put him to bed and turn his key in the door." As Owen stared an instant, apparently not understanding the motive of so much solicitude, he added: "Lechmere has a morbid curiosity about one of your legends—of your historic rooms. Nip it in the bud."

"Oh, the legend's rather good, but I'm afraid the room's an awful sell!" Owen laughed.

"You know you don't *believe* that, my boy!" young Lechmere exclaimed.

"I don't think he does," said Mr. Coyle, noticing Owen's mottled flush.

"He wouldn't try a night there himself!" young Lechmere pursued.

"I know who told you that," rejoined Owen, lighting a cigarette in an embarrassed way at the candle, without offering one to either of his companions.

"Well, what if she did?" asked the younger of these gentleman, rather red. "Do you want them *all* yourself?" he continued facetiously, fumbling in the cigarette-box.

Owen Wingrave only smoked quietly; then he exclaimed:

"Yes—what if she did? But she doesn't know," he added.

"She doesn't know what?"

"She doesn't know anything!—I'll tuck him in!" Owen went on gaily to Mr. Coyle, who saw that his presence, now that a certain note had been struck, made the young men uncomfortable. He was curious, but there was a kind of discretion, with his pupils, that he had always pretended to practise; a discretion that however didn't prevent him as he took his way upstairs from recommending them not to be donkeys.

At the top of the staircase, to his surprise, he met Miss Julian, who was apparently going down again. She had not begun to undress, nor was she perceptibly disconcerted at seeing him. She nevertheless, in a manner slightly at variance with the rigour with which she had overlooked him ten minutes before, dropped the words: "I'm going down to look for something. I've lost a jewel."

"A jewel?"

"A rather good turquoise, out of my locket. As it's the only ornament I have the honour to possess———!" And she passed down.

"Shall I go with you and help you?" asked Spencer Coyle.

The girl paused a few steps below him, looking back with her Oriental eyes.

"Don't I hear voices in the hall?"

"Those remarkable young men are there."

"*They'll* help me." And Kate Julian descended.

Spencer Coyle was tempted to follow her, but remembering his standard of tact he rejoined his wife in their apartment. He delayed however to go to bed, and though he went into his dressing-room he couldn't bring himself even to take off his coat. He pretended for half an hour to read a novel; after which, quietly, or perhaps I should say agitatedly, he passed from the dressing-room into the corridor. He followed this passage to the door of the room which he knew to have been assigned to young Lechmere and was comforted to see that it was closed. Half an hour earlier he had seen it standing open; therefore he could take for granted that the bewildered boy had come to bed. It was of this he had wished to assure himself, and having done so he was on the point of retreating. But at the same instant he heard a sound in the room—the occupant was doing, at the window, something which showed him that he might knock without the reproach of waking his pupil up. Young Lechmere came in fact to the door in his shirt and trousers. He admitted his visitor in some surprise, and when the door was closed again Spencer Coyle said:

"I don't want to make your life a burden to you, but I had it on my conscience to see for myself that you're not exposed to undue excitement."

"Oh, there's plenty of that!" said the ingenuous youth. "Miss Julian came down again."

"To look for a turquoise?"

"So she said."

"Did she find it?"

"I don't know. I came up. I left her with poor Wingrave."

"Quite the right thing," said Spencer Coyle.

"I don't know," young Lechmere repeated uneasily. "I left them quarrelling."

"What about?"

"I don't understand. They're a quaint pair!"

Spencer Coyle hesitated. He had, fundamentally, principles and scruples, but what he had in particular just now was a curiosity, or rather, to recognise it for what it was, a sympathy, which brushed them away.

"Does it strike you that *she's* down on him?" he permitted himself to inquire.

"Rather!—when she tells him he lies!"

"What do you mean?"

"Why, before *me*. It made me leave them; it was getting too hot. I stupidly brought up the question of the haunted room again, and said how sorry I was that I had had to promise you not to try my luck with it."

"You can't pry about in that gross way in other people's houses—you can't take such liberties, you know!" Mr. Coyle interjected.

"I'm all right—see how good I am. I don't want to go *near* the place!" said young Lechmere, confidingly. "Miss Julian said to me 'Oh, I daresay *you'd* risk it, but'—and she turned and laughed at poor Owen—'that's more than we can expect of a gentleman who has taken *his* extraordinary line.' I could see that something had already passed between them on the subject—some teasing or challenging of hers. It may have been only chaff, but his chucking the profession had evidently brought up the question of his pluck."

"And what did Owen say?"

"Nothing at first; but presently he brought out very quietly: 'I spent all last night in the confounded place.' We both stared and cried out at this and I asked him what he had seen there. He said he had seen nothing, and Miss Julian replied that he ought to tell his story better than that—he ought to make something good of it. 'It's not a story—it's a simple fact,' said he; on which she jeered at him and wanted to know why, if he had done it, he hadn't told her in the morning, since he knew what she thought of him. 'I know, but I don't care,' said Wingrave. This made her angry, and she asked him quite seriously whether he would care if he should know she believed him to be trying to deceive us."

"Ah, what a brute!" cried Spencer Coyle.

"She's a most extraordinary girl—I don't know what she's up to."

"Extraordinary indeed—to be romping and bandying words at that hour of the night with fast young men!"

Young Lechmere reflected a moment. "I mean because I think she likes him."

Spencer Coyle was so struck with this unwonted symptom of subtlety that he flashed out: "And do you think he likes *her*?"

But his interlocutor only replied with a puzzled sigh and a plaintive "I don't know—I give it up!—I'm sure he *did* see something or hear something," young Lechmere added.

"In that ridiculous place? What makes you sure?"

"I don't know—he looks as if he had. He behaves as if he had."

"Why then shouldn't he mention it?"

Young Lechmere thought a moment. "Perhaps it's too gruesome!"

Spencer Coyle gave a laugh. "Aren't you glad then *you're* not in it?"

"Uncommonly!"

"Go to bed, you goose," said Spencer Coyle, with another laugh. "But before you go tell me what he said when she told him he was trying to deceive you."

"'Take me there yourself, then, and lock me in!'"

"And *did* she take him?"

"I don't know—I came up."

Spencer Coyle exchanged a long look with his pupil.

"I don't think they're in the hall now. Where's Owen's own room?"

"I haven't the least idea."

Mr. Coyle was perplexed; he was in equal ignorance, and he couldn't go about trying doors. He bade young Lechmere sink to slumber, and came out into the passage. He asked himself if he should be able to find his way to the room Owen had formerly shown him, remembering that in common with many of the others it had its ancient name painted upon it. But the corridors of Paramore were intricate; moreover some of the servants would still be up, and he didn't wish to have the appearance of roaming over the house. He went back to his own quarters, where Mrs. Coyle soon perceived that his inability to rest had not subsided. As she confessed for her own part, in the dreadful place, to an increased sense of "creepiness," they spent the early part of the night in conversation, so that a portion of their vigil was inevitably beguiled by her husband's account of his colloquy with little Lechmere and by their exchange of opinions upon it. Toward two o'clock

Mrs. Coyle became so nervous about their persecuted young friend, and so possessed by the fear that that wicked girl had availed herself of his invitation to put him to an abominable test, that she begged her husband to go and look into the matter at whatever cost to his own equilibrium. But Spencer Coyle, perversely, had ended, as the perfect stillness of the night settled upon them, by charming himself into a tremulous acquiescence in Owen's readiness to face a formidable ordeal—an ordeal the more formidable to an excited imagination as the poor boy now knew from the experience of the previous night how resolute an effort he should have to make. "I hope he *is* there," he said to his wife: "it puts them all so in the wrong!" At any rate he couldn't take upon himself to explore a house he knew so little. He was inconsequent—he didn't prepare for bed. He sat in the dressing-room with his light and his novel, waiting to find himself nodding. At last however Mrs. Coyle turned over and ceased to talk, and at last too he fell asleep in his chair. How long he slept he only knew afterwards by computation; what he knew to begin with was that he had started up, in confusion, with the sense of a sudden appalling sound. His sense cleared itself quickly, helped doubtless by a confirmatory cry of horror from his wife's room. But he gave no heed to his wife; he had already bounded into the passage. There the sound was repeated—it was the "Help! help!" of a woman in agonised terror. It came from a distant quarter of the house, but the quarter was sufficiently indicated. Spencer Coyle rushed straight before him, with the sound of opening doors and alarmed voices in his ears and the faintness of the early dawn in his eyes. At a turn of one of the passages he came upon the white figure of a girl in a swoon on a bench, and in the vividness of the revelation he read as he went that Kate Julian, stricken in her pride too late with a chill of compunction for what she had mockingly done, had, after coming to release the victim of her derision, reeled away, overwhelmed, from the catastrophe that was her work—the catastrophe that the next moment he found himself aghast at on the threshold of an open door. Owen Wingrave, dressed as he had last seen him, lay dead on the spot on which his ancestor had been found. He looked like a young soldier on a battle-field.

THE END

Milton Keynes UK
Ingram Content Group UK Ltd.
UKHW030624061024
449204UK00004B/355